SOPHIE'S VOICE

Voices of Triumph Over Trauma

MARCIA GORANSON AND TOM JOSEPHSON

TRILOGY
A WHOLLY OWNED SUBSIDIARY OF **TBN**
PROFESSIONAL PUBLISHING MEETS POWERFUL PROMOTION

Sophie's Voice

Trilogy Christian Publishers
A Wholly Owned Subsidiary of Trinity Broadcasting Network
2442 Michelle Drive
Tustin, CA 92780

Copyright © 2024 by **Marcia Goranson and Tom Josephson**

10 9 8 7 6 5 4 3 2 1
Library of Congress Cataloging-in-Publication Data is available.
ISBN: 979-8-89333-317-6
ISBN: 979-8-89333-318-3

Sophie's Voice

Voices of Triumph over Trauma

Dedication

This work, this compilation is dedicated first of all to Tom's fifty-five family members that died in the ghettos and death camps of the Third Reich. To Tom's mother, Sophie, who escaped the Holocaust with her parents as a teenager. Also, to Jack Weisblack, a survivor of the Auschwitz concentration camp. Both were living inspirations to the power of the rejection of a victimhood mindset. They both lived and thrived in spite of the Evil determined to eliminate them.

The stories of both Sophie's and Jack's lives inspired me to move forward in my recovery from childhood devastation. I am determined to live and thrive as an overcomer. My past doesn't own me nor define me, but it happened. I live in the reality of redemption now, with the past as a memory as I look forward to the future and really live in the present.

With that in mind, this work is dedicated also to those who have loved and supported us through it all. Our spouses, our children and our friends. We love you all. Always.

Foreword

I have been a lover and follower of Jesus Christ for forty years. For about twenty of those years, I have been recovering from childhood sexual trauma and its effects. During that time, I wrote and published my first book in 2019.

That was the first time that I had 'gone public' with the truth about what happened to me as a child and how I had coped with the effects of the trauma as an adult. In the course of writing it, I was able to put pen to paper and scrape off the first layers of my embedded pain, processing as I went. It was a good place to start, a natural outcome of the progression in my healing journey.

I wasn't sure even then what I was really striving for. All I knew was that I had a compelling desire to recover my life and to be rid of the pain and confusion that still plagued me.

I met Tom during the sixty-third year of my life. I had been in recovery formally and had even had a life coach previous to Tom but there was still something missing and I didn't know what it was or how to find it.

Tom turned out to be incredibly intuitive. He also inspired and required real soul work out of me. My husband was incredibly supportive and participated in many hours of Tom's coaching as well.

What resulted after an intense few weeks was that I finally found the bottom drawer in my soul. I found where I had buried my outrage along with the shame I had carried for the perpetrator.

Shame is diabolically pervasive in the mental and emotional banks of a sexually traumatized child. I finally uncovered the real culprit of the confusion, apathy and my inability to fully live as my true self. Shame. Shame that was never mine to carry or hold. Shame was the main supporter of my real nemesis—self-loathing. Once I saw and realized the truth about how I had been deceived, my true self stood up.

I am now in the process of growing into my authentic self at long last. I've set down and given up the pretense that I maintained most of my life to protect those that betrayed and abandoned me, the ones that I loved the most.

As I continue to evolve into who I was created to be, I find that my anger at my betrayal is justified but I can let go of the life sentence that I once wanted to punish the betrayers with. As I grow more into myself, I also look more to the everlasting love and acceptance that I have received from my Good Shepherd, the one who always loved me and wanted me to walk and live closely with Him. By His grace my bitterness turns into mercy and my anger resolves into gratitude.

All of this has been facilitated by putting pen to paper once again. Much of my processing in the past months has come through what I have written. It just so happens that Tom, my life coach, friend, and older brother that I never had, is also an author. He and I have collaborated on a book, a work of our writings called *Sophie's Voice-Voices of Triumph over Trauma*. Together we are voicing our struggles and the overcoming of them by the same grace that brought us together.

Acknowledgments…to Ryan Goranson, my son, who Tom has designated the 'Canary in the Soul Mine.'

Cover art by…. Natacha Villamia Sochat

Table of Contents

PART ONE

SOPHIE'S VOICE

written by Tom Josephson unless stated
otherwise.

INTRODUCTION TO PART ONE

I am grateful to my cousin, Debbie Christa, for asking me to comment on telling some of my mother's story as a Holocaust survivor as inspiration to me and others in overcoming a "victim" mindset. Why? Debbie asked about it primarily because I have become a follower of Jesus Christ.

Debbie's concern raises a significant issue, so I will take the opportunity to make a very simple but important distinction. Mom's family, my family, were slaughtered by Nazi Germany during the Holocaust, because of the perverse, twisted, wicked race theory of the Nazi Reich, not because of Judaism as a religious faith. "Jewish" can refer to cultural identity, ethnicity (like a blood line) and religion. There are Jews who are atheists who would be regarded, and who regard themselves, as Jews. Whereas with another faith, one might say "I was raised in the church," but consider myself an atheist. In that case identity is viewed as a different thing from faith. But Judaism is seen as both, ethnicity, and faith.

Below is a direct citation from the US Holocaust Museum website:

"The Nazis defined Jews by race, not religion. They claimed that Jews belonged to a separate race. They also claimed that

Jews were inferior to all other races. The Nazi definition of Jews included people who did not practice Judaism."

As you can see this was an attack on people who were ethnically Jews by blood, whether they (we) practiced the faith or not. Actually, there was no religious observance in my immediate family. In fact, my father stated that he was an atheist. My grandparents never discussed religion with me either; yet they suffered as surely as the most pious.

I am a proud descendant of Jews. I have never renounced my identity; nor will I. Rather, I have found Faith and purpose in striving to perfect my walk in my Christian faith. But if the Nazis were to re-emerge, I would be hauled off to the death camps and ghettos just like my family was.

Sophie's story is not about her religious faith, my conversion, or leading anyone to God. It is about her, the overcomer. We respect Sophie's faith. We honor Mom's stand of triumph over trauma! Sophie's story, her voice, has inspired many people of all ages, genders, faiths, ethnic, and cultural backgrounds who have heard it from me or others repeating what they have heard. That is one of the inspiring voices of the book. I urge you to experience for yourself the inspiration and the lessons of Sophie and other voices who have overcome trauma and abuse.

Our purpose is to inspire, create hope, and offer some things we have learned from our prices paid.

GO SOPHIE

The first time I heard Sophie's story I was struck by both the awesomeness and the heartbreak of it. I was born near the tail end of the Baby Boomer generation but I of course knew many women born in her time. We call them the Greatest Generation in the US because they endured both the Great Depression and World War Two. They are also called the Silent Generation.

Imagine living through two major world crises during the course of your childhood and early adulthood. Imagine now being female during those years. In terms of life choices, it was very different for women then...how did Sophie respond to the choices she had? Her family escaped certain death when the Nazis were taking trainloads of innocent people to concentration death camps. Fortuitously, they escaped and she and her family lived relatively normal lives in New York City.

She claimed that she was not a victim since so many had suffered so much more than she. I believe that yes, she buried the truth about the trauma she endured and how it affected her. She made a hard choice—as most women in her generation were accustomed to making. She chose to live as an overcomer in spite of what her circumstances had been. Was she untrue to herself? Perhaps most assuredly. I see her decision as an opportunity to live her life out of gratitude and not in a perpetual state of victimhood. She didn't label herself a victim.

Sophie's attitude spoke to me concerning my own trauma and the choices I have today that she didn't have. I have the opportunity to speak out loud, to process out loud and to heal out loud. I can speak for myself and for others who have no voice or have had their voices muted.

I believe that if Sophie were here today that she would say to me—'Yes. Use your voice. Stand up to your enemy! I stood up silently and showed the evil that it did not win because I went forward with my life. I might have been victimized but it didn't define me. It's not who I was.'

So, in honor of Sophie I will say NO to evil. What happened to me does not define me. I will be who I was created to be, born to be. Go Sophie!

What Sophie Said

What Mom said in the handwritten pages she left revealed her innermost feelings to me for the first time. In the quote below, Mom (Sophie) talks about a date October 20, 1938. That night at 2 a.m., the Gestapo (Secret State Police of Germany) arrested my Grandfather, and with no justification deported him out of Germany to Poland. He and my Grandmother had moved to Berlin from Lodz (pronounced Ludge) Poland. My Grandfather and all male citizens of Poland were rounded up within thirty minutes all over Germany. Many Poles had emigrated to Germany to make a better life. They were there with the legal status of work visas. Berlin was the commercial and cultural center of Europe at that time. Poland, with its history of Antisemitism, would not let the Jews back in. They were placed in camps on the Polish/German border.

"October 20,1938 was the most traumatic day in my life. It is hard for me to put into words the pain and fear and hopelessness I felt at that time. For many, many years I refused to have a phone in the bedroom. I was afraid of a ringing phone at night. I was haunted by these memories."

This is the most intimate conversation I ever had with my Mother. But it didn't happen until ten years after she died when I found the handwritten pages she had left for me.

It was "pain and fear and hopelessness" Mom kept locked up under the cool, perfect exterior the world knew as Sophie.

Had I thought about it, I could have, I should have, sought out my mother, as a real person. Maybe she just didn't want to reveal her pain to me while she was alive, or maybe I could have helped her face those fears and find herself, who she was, and her voice, and she could have been the voice, for the fifty-five dead in her family…

But Mom chose it this way: The way of "Nothing"

"Nothing much happened to me. What right do I have to feel like I suffered when so many had it worse?"

For most of my life, I thought Mom was minimizing due to survivor's guilt, but I have come to believe she was claiming victory over the Nazi Reich…I believe Mom showed the world the assault on the Jewish People failed, that they couldn't slow her down from her destiny, of building a great life, a great career as an advertising executive, manifesting dignity and poise and elegance in all situations, a great mom, a great wife, a patron of the arts, a stunning, vibrant artist in her own right, a great cook, a great friend…

She stood tall and gave the lie to every lie the Nazis told. Her magnificence was in her willingness to show the world strength and honor in the face of the most wicked even at the expense of her own voice.

She kept her feelings hidden. She paid the price of never knowing her true self! But she refused to yield her dignity! Mom knew I would lift up who she really was...She knew I would become her voice, and so, I offer to history, to God, and to you *Sophie's Voice*!

Sophie's Voice

My name is Sophie and I have something to say.
Now that I'm good and dead,
and you can't kill me anymore,
you can't scare me anymore,
and I'm no longer a child growing up a Jew in Nazi Germany,
the voice I never had
can be heard.

I am in the same ground as my family,
my grandparents, aunts, uncles and cousins,
who died in the death camps and ghettos
of the third Reich,
with no notice,
no graves,
no bodies,
no children,
no legacy.

That ground is Mother Earth.
She drank our blood,
and now she is my resting place.
I am that little girl who got kicked out of public school at thirteen
years of age,

who was required to say "Heil Hitler!" to my teachers
before they killed us.

I am that little girl
who saw the billboards all over Berlin
spreading lies about my people,
images of dark, hook-nosed monsters drinking blood.

I am that teenage girl
who heard the Gestapo bang on our door in Berlin,
at two am of an October morning,
and saw my father
dragged out of bed and kicked out of the country
for no reason.

I am that teenage girl
who saw mobs in the streets below
destroy my parents' business,
smash the world they built,
smash the glass in businesses and synagogues
all across Germany,
then blame us for what they did,
and steal everything.
You call it "Kristallnacht,"
but I was there.
It didn't have the solemnity of a name.
I was crying to my mother,
"Mommy, we won't get out of here alive,"
as I looked out the window

and saw the mobs looking for us,
looking for Jews to blame and kill.

I am that teenage girl
who escaped the killing
of my uncles and aunts and grandparents
and all the children,
fifty-five in all in my family.
They tore us apart,
starved us,
beat us,
gassed us,
shot us,
buried us in pits,
tortured the children and infirm
for no reason other than madness born of lies.
I am Zofia Lieberman!
I have died twice.
I died as a girl.
I was dead, my true self
never lived,
but I surrounded the walking dead soul in me
in a good life in America;
and when I died in the flesh,
I was a mother and a grandmother.

I never knew who I was,
but my son read my words

in a document I left among his photographs,
and he is articulating them to you now.

They killed so many of us,
but my son was given life and a voice;
and you can't shut him up.

And though I may be dead two times over,
my voice has now been heard.
My people can rest now.
We have lived!
I am Sophie.
I lived!

EMPTINESS

Rudy Kocinski, our distant cousin,
the one you adored,
lived in your brown leather photo album,
the album that muted the sounds of our home in the 1950's and
60's.

Tall and handsome Rudy was.
Underground he went,
in Brussels,
after you and Grandma escaped Germany into Brussels,
after Kristallnacht,
out of hiding
and slipped out of Germany,
having been in receipt of visas procured miraculously
by Uncle Joe,
and mailed documents and money to Grandpa,
in a camp on the Polish border,
after he had been dragged out of your home in the middle of the
night,
and kicked out of Germany, being Jewish and a citizen of Poland,
and one day, he miraculously appeared at the train station in
Brussels,

and you left for Cuba at seventeen,
but Rudy, without a visa, stayed.

Like a caged animal
he must have paced the floor at night,
you must have thought,
perhaps thinking of you,
feeling blood flowing through his thighs,
itching to burst into the world,
but biding his time.

His tall frame must have been cramped,
you must have thought,
looking through tear-misted eyes
at the brittle pages
bound in brown leather,
while Dad kept us away,
kept us quiet.

Rudy's sister, Eva, disappeared.
I can see you dwell on the picture of them both,
handsome, strolling along a great boulevard in cosmopolitan
Berlin,
before the Nazi infection became fatal,
and I see your hand tremble still,
holding the page corner between thumb and forefinger,
about to move on,
but stuck in the pain, and fear of the past,
flaring up as if happening now,

as the handsome, tall and vital Rudy,
he of the brown leather photo album,
went back into the silence of the turned page and shut album,
went back into eternity,
as surely as he walked out of hiding one day,
for some unknown reason,
and disappeared off the face of the earth.

And I remember your sigh
as you reverently closed the brown leather covers,
composed yourself
for another year or so,
closed yourself,
silent and shut and neatly put away.

This is the legacy you kept inside,
this is the album we opened after your funeral,
and this time,
though I never wanted your story to end,
the album is shut by my own hand,
Rudy goes back to oblivion.

And as I finish this little history,
I feel the emptiness
as surely as you did,

I feel the emptiness
of inherited pain,
pausing with my mind trembling like your fingers once did,
over the memory I am closing,

the memory, the emptiness,

of never again seeing you

close the brown leather photo album, wipe your eyes,

and sigh.

SORROW

I went shopping today
In the clear light of winter

Surrounded by sorrow,
As cool, bright lines
Bounced off the roads,

My mother died last week
And I miss her today,
Getting back out into the world,

I never expected this day
Of detachment
Never realized I'd be alone,
Never thought her will would leave Earth

And somehow, I would have to conjure it
For myself, as best I can,

But the gap is too big to ignore
And I guess I'm too weak
And her will was stronger than I knew
Her love was bigger and more pervasive
I see now
Too late!

Oh no, I missed it!
I missed it in my anguish
My anger and guilt,
My ongoing obsession
With my father's cruelty

It took this subtraction
For me to see the missing whole
The entity that has departed,
The totality I see now
So much larger than my capacity

But how could I know?
Mom, please come back
Tell me what to make of this,
Help me heal
Help me love you
Alive
Like I miss you now

LOOKING OUT FROM THE SCHOOLYARD

Looking out from the schoolyard in The Bronx,
a teenager, full of life,
full of fight,
I can remember my mother
walking elegantly
right to left on this Bronx street,
coming home from work,
walking, gracefully,
as her parents and so many others had walked
up and down the boulevards of The Bronx and Brooklyn,
Holocaust survivors, putting on their Sunday best,
window shopping the local stores,
trying to regain their sense of dignity and self-worth,
to block out whatever horror
they escaped and left behind.

And she had escaped much horror,
my mother had,
but I never knew,
never knew there was terror inside her,
never knew The Holocaust was lodged inside her,
images of the chain link fences of the Ghettos and concentration

camps
she had escaped, and were banished from her consciousness,
were still firmly rooted deep in her sub-conscious.

She walked past the schoolyard with its chain link fence,
the image of her deepest fears,
but she ignored it, banished it, denied its reality,
which is why she didn't notice me,
often times no more than five feet from her
as she strode down this Bronx street.

Yet, I was trying to understand my own life.

On my side of the fence,
I saw the dignified, heroic woman everyone saw;
but I wanted my Mom,
I wanted her to see me
to help me understand I was okay,
that my father was an angry man,
that the intensity of his anger wasn't about me,
though it was directed at me,
that I didn't deserve it.

I got unconditional support from my grandmother,
otherwise, I don't think I would have made it through.
But I still wanted, I needed that validation from Mom,
or, even better, her defending me sometimes
when Dad seemed out of control.

So, my friends might say
"TJ, your mom's coming,"
and I would lean forward against the chain link fence,
the fence that kept us apart,
the adults and us.
My hands would loosely hold the fence;
my friends would stop dribbling,
stop shooting basketballs,
and would laugh, as I smiled,
as my mother, day after day,
walked the streets of Berlin in her mind,
into Manhattan,
and back home to The Bronx,
away from the nightmare her childhood had been,
away from the death camps and ghettos,
away from the images strewn with starving children,
the images of her cousins, her aunts and uncles,
and grandparents,
away from the ovens and other chambers of death,
and the murder of her family,
not even twenty-five years past,
and I, I didn't really know.

I didn't know the very streets upon which she walked,
my beautiful, sophisticated mother,
walking right towards me
smiling serenely

and passing right to left
oblivious.

We would laugh, my friends and I.
Parents are so odd!
laughing that my own mother
would pass so close, and not notice,
day after day,
though sometimes, I would say "Hey, Mom!"
and she would turn slowly
as she walked by
and say "Hi dear"
and it was all a dream.
Today it is forty-five years since those days in the schoolyard,
Mom's stride is slowed by neuropathy,
but her entrance into the rehab center in Florida,
is still pure class,
as she looks after my father, sliding into Alzheimer's
and emphysema decay.

And as Mom and I talk
Mom's feelings of willful, creative, survival-related denial,
which she needed to keep completely sealed,
and my feelings of lack of validation,
still separate us.

The unspoken meanings of the images lodged inside us,
the chain link fence of my schoolyard,
and the chain link fence of the ghetto and camps

she denies were real to her,
keep me here,
and her there,
as if the fence were still between us.

I know this now.
I regret not seeing this duality
not celebrating it all when Mom was alive.

Coaching Marcia to press through the effects of childhood incest
has expanded my own understanding.
One of the major goals of this book
is to help others avoid the regret
by seeing what we have learned
from our experience,
and from the lessons of overcomers
like Mom, Jack Weisblack,
who you will meet soon,
and two or three others.
I encourage you, to use what I have learned
in my seventy-three years
to keep pushing until you are free.

THE BUTTERfly OF BERLIN

I came to the rehab early
to be with Mom,
and saw her in bed
disguised as an old woman,

and the sight of her breaking down
was in stark contrast to my image of my mother,
the overcomer, the woman who coiled herself
into a cocoon of willful, creative denial.

She insisted she was not a victim of the Holocaust,
despite fifty-five dead in her family,
dead in the ghetto of Lodz (pronounced Ludge), Poland,
or dead in the concentration camps.

Mom rejected the stance of victimhood.
Instead, she chose to live a great life,
of dignity, sophistication and kindness.

After a miraculous escape from Germany, and Europe,
Mom went about the business of coiling her cocoon.
She learned flawless English at nineteen,
notwithstanding that linguists say it can't be done,
not without some accent;

but Mom had no detectable accent.
She earned a degree and studied business,
eventually becoming a vice president
of a prominent Madison Avenue advertising agency.

She was admired by young and old alike,
both professionally and in our family.
There was no pretense in her.
There was fear and pain locked up deep inside,
but no pretense.

Mom wore her cocoon with style and elan.
She married, had children,
had subscriptions to the Metropolitan Opera,
and the New York Philharmonic symphony,
at Lincoln Center,
went to Shakespeare in the Park
had company box seats to the US Open Tennis tournament,
frequented the world class Museums in New York,
dined in some of the best restaurants in the world,
bought a condo and retired in Delray Beach Florida,
travelled to see me in Oregon and Texas, at least yearly,
went to New York twice a year,
travelled the world,
became a gourmet cook,
a stunning, vibrant artist, a painter,
gave my sister a wedding at the Plaza Hotel,
all that, she did, with my father, who had a good job
as a warehouse manager,

but, certainly not nearly enough to create their lifestyle.
It was Mom's income that underwrote their lifestyle,
and her profit-sharing plan funded the bulk of their retirement.

She did that!

After starting her life here as a nineteen-year-old immigrant,
whose bank account was frozen because of her German citizenship
during World War Two!

And I never saw her lose her composure!
Never!
No one did.

Through it all
she was a loving and dutiful daughter, niece, and cousin,
handling all the paperwork
her parents couldn't manage.

She did all this in her second language,
on her own initiative,

and had to come to grips with the death of all her grandparents,
and most of her uncles and aunts and cousins,
fifty-five dead, but you couldn't tell
by her demeanor, or how she talked;
she had the pain and grief and fear and shame sealed tight inside!

She created this masterpiece of a life,
a triumph over trauma
because that was her will!

People were drawn to her,
to her unfazed style,
for she was unfazed.

But tonight, her cocoon cracked
and she began to burst forth,
after staring at her dinner
for several minutes,
with her napkin reflexively,
appropriately placed in her lap,
she just stared and I could see the end was near.

Here, on the gurney,
as her magnificent life wound down,
she began to speak in soft low tones.

At first, I thought she was muttering and confused,
but I realized her barely audible words
revealed the German accent she had kept under wraps
all these years.

That was when it hit me what a mighty warrior Mom was!
How much effort, discipline, focus and commitment
she revealed in those moments.

Mom passed through life
in her own elegant, triumphant way.

Her soul is tired,
tired of holding tight her cocoon
so properly all this time.

I appreciate, I admire, I marvel at the gift of her creation,
the elegance and compassion,
and iron strong will,
that was my mother.

Her wings have grabbed the air
and she is soaring now,
soaring over the fluttering commotion,
unfurling for us all.

Mom stopped to hover in this world,
beautifully unfurled,
long enough to sip some love,
and now she is gone.

Mom Walks on By

It was a miracle they got out of Germany,
to Cuba, then America,
away from the Holocaust,
from the hatred,
from being an outcast,
away from the past,
she was young and beautiful,
walk on by.

And she married an American,
a passionate man,
a damaged soul, an abused orphan,
who felt her pain,
and more,
felt his own,
and they married,
and merged,
walk on by.

And she bore my sister and me,
and, believing a woman never gave the lie
to her man's will,
no matter what,

no matter the fury in furrowed brows,
no matter the relentless, furious criticism
like an assault on her son's soul
she didn't notice,
just like she didn't acknowledge the horrors of the Holocaust.
Walk on by.

The desolation is complete,
it is my fifty-ninth year,
and I know now,
though I admire your stance,
Mom, you weren't able to be present for me
after childhood.
Walk on by.

My mother escaped the Nazis physically,
and constructed her life,
like listening to "Walk on By"
day after day after day.

She loved her husband
loved her idea of family,
but with no tears shed,
my mother walked by,
never knew my pain
and I never knew hers.
Walk on by.

Mom walked by
the schoolyard where I played ball,

not seeing me most days,
not seeing me as I was ever.
And I never knew her as she was,
and neither did she!

Mom told me, when she was eighty-eight years old,
"I don't know who I am"

It is a tragic price she paid,
to maintain composure and elegance
in the face of evil,
but she did it!

Sophie took a lifelong stand for dignity, grace, excellence
and kindness and defeated the Nazi race theory
by how she lived her life!

I'm proud of my Mother, Sophie,
even if some of the cost was passed down to me,
even if I had to excavate myself from tunnels of pain and shame.

I say good for you Mom!
You walked through this world beautifully, magnificently!
Walk on by, Mom.
Walk on by.

I love you,
I will see you on the other side.

PART TWO

TOM'S STRUGGLE

written by Tom Josephson unless stated
otherwise.

The previous section about Sophie is generally from my perspective as an adult. Before I matured, processed my issues, and gained insight, I struggled. This section describes that period, from childhood through much of my early adulthood, a period of darkness and searching. I left my parent's house. The pressure I felt from my father was intense.

I had no defense.

One of the unfortunate effects of sustained anger, rage, screaming and criticism, where there is no or minimal supportive, corrective feedback, is the capacity of the child to continue to make some sense, or to feel safe and secure, that capacity is compromised. The child sometimes separates himself from his experience by feeling as if he is not in his own body and mind. This is called dissociation. It can become an automatic response to intense feelings.

In the following pieces, I describe what that feeling is like, and, in "My Decoder Ring," I describe how the process of dissociation impacts the thinking, and self-image of the child, as he tries to reason through it. Faulty understanding creates beliefs that are untrue, and ways of being and feeling that are ineffective, and irrational, and which lead to chaotic relationships.

Out of the chaos, something miraculous occurred. "The Doorman" is the pivotal piece of my struggle. Things changed!

THE COUNCIL

The Council sat cross-legged in a semi-circle around a campfire
not far from this remote pristine lake
nestled near the Berkshire Mountains.
They faced the dining hall,
volleyball and basketball courts,
and paths that wandered into the woods
to the stables, or the lake or the cabins,
and, also faced, on the sloped field,
one hundred-thirty campers and staff.

As the summer sun dipped behind the trees,
backlit by the crackling fire,
the four pledges stood on the crest of the ridge,
facing the boys and men of the camp.

This was the high point of the weekly campfires of the Council,
this secret, most-high society,
fully garbed like the Sioux and Cherokee
who had once called these lands home.

There were songs, stories, tales of trips into town,
weekly honors, and this final induction
of these four honored and prestigious pledges,

one of whom was just thirteen,
the youngest camper ever chosen.

And now the anticipated moment had arrived.

There was a quiet that covered the evening,
as the eyes of the young campers stared in wonder,
others in yearning,
and the counselors and staff smiled,
as, in the dusk-dim light,
the head of the Council called the first young man to step forward,
then lit the peace pipe and passed it around the Council,
each in turn, musing, then puffing on the pipe as a symbol of
acceptance.

After the first three pledges had been accepted into the Council,
the thirteen-year-old stood alone, facing the camp,
with the Council seated cross-legged behind.
He thought how alien it all seemed,
to be a city boy from the projects of the Bronx
among (as he saw it) these "privileged" suburbanites,
and how strange to be a pledge,
and all the silliness it entailed,
culminating in twenty-four hours of silence,
and how his rebellious, insecure nature couldn't abide.

And as I stood alone on the crest of the ridge,
illuminated by the last rays of the setting sun
and the faint orange glow of the dying fire behind,
a sense of impending doom filled my spirit,

and I went to a place I knew all too well,
accustomed as I was to my father's rage.

I left my body, standing tall and stoic,
withdrew to an inner place,
where I became a numb witness to my own rejection,
and noticed the stunned gasps,
"Oh my God! They won't take the pipe!
Can you believe it? They're not letting him in!"

I heard the Council members rise, and walk away,
Including the three accepted inductees,
and so, I was completely alone.

The campers dispersed.
Three or four counselors and waiters came up to me,
and said they were proud that I took it like a man.

Whatever or whoever anyone thought they saw that evening,
It wasn't me.
I was gone,
but the memory of that sense of doom, standing alone on a rise,
has remained for a lifetime,
portending other arrows about to pierce my heart and soul.

And to this day, now nearly sixty years hence
I can't tell you exactly where that broken boy went.

THE MINER WHO
SEARCHED FOR HIMSELF

His miner's hat sat atop his head its light throwing a big cone into the darkness framing the world he saw: reality was inside the cone and nothing else was real. Try as he might he could never see himself, for upon removing his hat he saw only the light, never himself or the world, just a hat with a light on it; and there was no seeing inside for how can you see backwards from darkness into light?

Sometimes, I would find myself uncaved in broad daylight like the others of my species. Then kaleidoscopes would appear magically and mysterious colors flooded my eyes. These sunlit days were beautiful, filled with the music of life; filling all my senses but not the miner in me.

I lost track of him years ago after he withdrew back to his cave to begin his search anew.

I am a miner. I search in vain to see with my own eyes.

So, This Is My Life

So, this is it,
this is my life,
a lifelong exercise in covert operations,
full of shadows that materialize unannounced,
and slink into the darkness
before I can figure out who or what they are.

This is it,
layers of my self
emerge and disappear
before I notice,
keeping several steps ahead of my awareness,

unless I talk to another,
and that attention focuses me
into responding,
and suddenly
I see myself
as in a mirror.

Fully, I can describe what I then see
can see inside with that light,
and feel the warmth,

the clarity, the wholeness
that I see reflected.

Until the light dims
and I am alone with myself,
and the wholeness crumbles
into chaos.

And the chaos moves
like a kaleidoscope in front of my eyes,
like crowd noise muffling the truth
from reaching my ears.

And I alone must survive
this most intricate combat zone,
where demons can morph into parents,
and evaporate like mist in the light,
when outsiders appear.

Body parts float in the void,
but somehow you hold on.
I held on,
holding on,
my stomach,
my bowels,
anxious to stay out of trouble.
This is serious.
This is my life.

This is deception,
illusion,
feelings that fly through me
like nightmares,
everything unnamed.

A puppet is born.
Welcome to my world.
This is my life.
This,
my life,
is all there is.
This is it.

This is my one and only life
and you have graced me with caring,
my one and only me.
Ain't life grand?

My Manic Addict

My manic addict got loose again and did his thing,
used me, tossed me into his fire and left.
And he's laughing!
Laughing on the other side of security
while I crawl through the airport.

He can't get me anymore, for now,
but it's too late,
I'm desperately broke and corrupted.

I'm at the gate now,
waiting for my plane to take me back from Vegas,
but my pocket and my soul are empty.
He stole them in broad daylight,
after telling me he would for months.

My manic addict got loose alright.
He lured my mind into a trance,
spun me around. put blinders on me,
and dropped me, his fool,
in front of a craps table.
The rest is history.
It's time to bury him
and my "should haves" and "could haves,"

It's time to take a stand
against that shrew!

Wait my manic addict is waving!
I think I heard him say from his smirking mouth,
"goodbye for now, see you soon!"

No, I know he said it!
My manic addict and I both know
he has new plans for me.

Now, for whatever it's worth,
So do you!

THE DOORMAN

On Fifth Avenue well-heeled women
would get out of my cab
and stroll to the entry
of their elegant residence.
They would be greeted
by a man in a green uniform,
with hat and white gloves.
He would open the door,
and they would disappear
inside opulent shadows.

Part II

Twenty-five years ago
while I was meditating,
I transformed,
sprouted eagle's wings
and rose up on an escalator into the clouds,
poised for whatever awaited me.

I rose off the top,
and soared, not just over the land,
but back through time,
and saw my ancestral generations

down below,

working fields, carting goods from town to town,

maybe dodging an Inquisitor,

or sharing stories of Charlemagne

or Atilla the Hun,

now in ancient Rome

where the Apostles did their work,

and further back past

Alexander and the Persians,

and came to ground at Sinai.

Part III

It looked like a music festival,

except around the many tens of thousands of campfires,

there was calm.

So, I strolled through,

and saw Joshua.

his eyes reflected majesty and hope.

We said hello and talked briefly,

but he turned to scold a child

running too close to the fire.

As I walked,

I heard many conversations

like ours,

ordinary people experiencing

extraordinary things.

Part IV

I came to the tabernacle.
Its magnificence astonished the barren ground,
and I understood why
the book of Numbers is so detailed,
revealing awe, love, and gratitude in each
stitch and carving.

Inside, the altar was in plain view.
There were dried blood stains on the altar itself,
and on the ground upon which it sat.

I found the Holy of Holies
at the rear and reached my hand out
to open the curtain and partake
of the Presence.

In that instant everything disappeared completely,
and I was back in my living room,
sitting on the floor,
meditating,
humbled.
I was not in charge,
and glad of it,
did not know why,
as a human, I was excluded.
We are all excluded.

But then again,
I didn't create the universe,
or life, or anything.

Part V

I am descended from Jewish Holocaust survivors and victims.
There were fifty-five dead in my mother's family.
I was and am their legacy...

Twenty-five years later,
my wife at the time
asked me to go with her to church,
having been raised by a preacher.

The Church was alive,
and awakened something in me.

Part VI

One afternoon, suddenly, I was back at Sinai.
Joshua and the others
were exactly as they had been
when I first walked among them,
as if one, and only one, instant
had passed.

I was in the Tabernacle,
exactly as I had been
the instant before,
twenty-five human years later.

I was still facing the Holy of Holies,
contemplating the glory of God,
still seeking His Presence,
resigned, to the separation,
but grateful
for the undeserved blessings
bestowed on my frail humanity.

Part VII

To my amazement, a green-uniformed arm
reached out from behind the curtain of separation,
which then began to open.

Jesus revealed Himself,
son of man, and Son of God,
and welcomed me in,
with a smile and extended hand,

as if He were dressed in a green coat,
replete with hat and white gloves,
a doorman to Glory,
a bridge out of separation,
the Redeemer out of Human limitation,
Perfector of Creation.

I realized Jesus literally IS the way,
makes a way out of no way.
Where no human can access,
HE is there.

The following Sunday
I acknowledged and accepted Him,
and His Sacrifice on the Cross,
and consequent Resurrection.

I was baptized in water,
made my public affirmation,
unworried what my people would say,
when they saw through death
my conversion.

I know now
the multiplied undeserved blessings
of life, and life eternal
with the Creator, in all His Glory,
with His Son, Jesus Christ,
and led by the Holy Spirit,

and I have never again
felt abandoned in the moment to moment,
or felt separated or alone again.

Response to The Doorman

by Marcia Goranson

The miracle of His manifest presence! The awesomeness of it is beyond description but it is captured here, for you and I. For all of us! Tom, your willingness to share this utterly magnificent, extremely personal moment is so important and moving. He, the Lord, your Doorman, longs to be close to us and this testimony proves it in real time! Thank you!

My Decoder Ring

Everyone seemed to know what to do,
but it all looked too complicated
for me to sort through,
so, I sat and waited
at the escalator
where shoppers rose as if with wings
toting bags filled with gifts
and other things they knew to buy...

but how did they know?

Everyone seemed to know what to do,
in the morning when I went to school
grownups everywhere passed through us
waiting for the school bus
on their way to the job
they knew well how to do...

but how did they know?

Who built the schools?
Who told them what to wear?
Who told their parents' parents
to pet the dog but not a bear?

Everyone knew who was who
and with a certainty
what to do
or so it seemed…

but how did they know?

What was it they all knew?
When the nature of it all
was sin and chaos
from Adam's fall from grace
the human race was disgraced
yet still they knew…

but how did they know?

Inside of me was fear
and the answer to my father's question,
what's wrong with you?
What's wrong with you?

The chaos and fear were real
and so too was
"There's something wrong with me"
I wish I knew
just like all of you
know the monster that must live inside you too
since mine was real
my father told me
then yours was too

yet all of you know what to do
why not me?

I must be worse then
than all of you…

you must have some key or ring
or some other thing or two
I know it now,
and I know too,
whatever it was
was given to you

so, this I know
what's wrong with me
is wrong with you
but you found out
and it all worked out
and then whatever it was must have left all of you
for all of you know what to do
yet I still sit in shame
while you all get jobs and kids and stuff
buy houses, live lives and write books

it's all out of reach for me
where was my key?

I must be so bad
it was withheld from me
by father and mother

and since father saw it well
he rightly kept my secret
buried inside me
heaped his anger and his shame
into me
I was to blame

It wasn't you
you got your key or other thing
that was withheld from me
since it must be true

I must be worse than all of you
so, I had to lie
and pretend I felt just like you
a proud key bearing ex shamed monster
you locked away to become worthy
of love and God and all the rest
you knew to do

but not me,

I had to lie
I had to pretend
the monster inside me
was as gone as yours was from you

so as bad as you all must have been too
I was worse
rejected as a reject

that's how I grew
to find a ring or some other thing or two

because the key to kill the monster
was no longer there
I have to carry this shame everywhere

I'm not worth even the trinket of a key
given everyone else
but withheld from me

So, I became as beast of a man!
I will beat you every way I can
you will never see the beast
that sucked the soul out of me
and replaced the "keyless" beast who had no key

So, I surmised the key was no longer available to me,
but still maybe a ring or other thing
will fix what's wrong with me
that you would plainly see
if you could see what he well knew
I am so much worse
than all of you
whose parents with pride and love
could stomach you long enough
to find your key

but never me

but it's all ok
there must be a ring
a decoder ring
I guess for me

Then Jesus reached his arm to me
and showed the Way
for me to see
and I saw Glory was there for me
He covered me as well as you
and now I'm born again in Him

I'm not alone
I'm His child too
In Him I'm worthy
In Him I'm whole
In Him I'm redeemed
Through Him is the Way
to Eternal love with God, the Father
with the Holy Spirit
and Jesus Christ the Shephard
Who found me

And that splintered song of a self is done.

Thank you, Lord.

To My Family Murdered in the Holocaust

To my family murdered in The Holocaust,
this is my testimony to you:

I am descended from the same blood
that was drained from your starved, gassed and burned bodies
by the death-dealing Nazi cancer
that metastasized out of Germany in the 1930's.

Our ancestors were at Sinai with Moses,
or represented there,
when God decreed his covenant
with us, the Jews.

And we lived as Jews for three thousand two hundred years,
covered and excoriated for the covenant's sake,
but always identified both by blood and faith,
unyielding, until
revitalizing in freedom here
in America and Israel.

Sometimes people would ask
about my relationship with Jesus, and if I could accept Him
as Who He says He is,

to which I would say,
if He revealed Himself to me, and I could see
for myself, then how could I say no.

The truth is I never had a relationship with God,
or Who He was,
and never knew how to pray heart-felt to
the Unamenable, the Giver of life,
the Source of love, justice and compassion,
the Creator or everything that was, is and ever will be.
How do you relate to an abstract reality
Who cannot be named or imaged?

So, through the years, I vacillated between agnostic
and the receiver of blessings
from some Unknown Blesser,

yet remained loyal to our blood,
by culture and identity, a Jew,
but marginal in faith in the Almighty.

Years of contemplation, education and meditation
yielded the same fruit:
loyal, grateful,
but alone.

And then the Messiah revealed Himself to me in the flesh,
the same flesh that was pierced and crucified to death as a man,
but then restored to perfection, life eternal and glory,
as the only begotten Son of God the Father,

the God of the Covenant,

who sought and achieved relationship with man,

through Jesus's blood sacrifice as atonement for human sin,

atonement for my sin and sin nature,

and restoration to worthiness of connection with God

through Jesus, Lord and Savior, and Gate opener of the pathway to
eternal life in Paradise,

and further, the Holy Spirit came to dwell as God in me,

and so, I was baptized in water attended by the Holy Spirit,

and accepted Jesus as my Lord and Savior,

through Whom I am forgiven of my sin,

and washed in His blood.

Now I can pray from the heart as well as my mind,

and can enter the Promised Land of Eternal Life,

through Jesus's sacrifice,

but there is more:

I pray I can serve as your surrogate.

We had surrogates at Sinai receiving the covenant on our behalf
before we were born, and now, I ask the Almighty for me to be
your surrogate,

receiving the Sacrifice and New Covenant through Jesus
after your death.

Do not be afraid.

In no way does my conversion repudiate or diminish
your lives, deaths or sacrifices,
nor does it void Moses and God's covenant with the Jews.

Rather, I pray, through the Creative Power of the Holy Spirit,
the Covenant written in the blood of Jesus
can flow miraculously back to cover you through my conversion.

In any case, consider accepting this as glorification and illumination
out of the dark unknown death of the concentration camps
and starved, frozen death of the ghettos.

MY SHAME

My shame was invisible to me for a long time
it distorted my thoughts and feelings
and drove me to isolation

When I first spoke of it
I felt like I was free falling from an airplane
It was very uncomfortable.

I identified it with a hideous rabbit's foot I bought,
boney, lightly stained purple
I put it on a key chain

Keeping my shame out and visible
seemed to help
but after a while I stopped being aware of it

so, it grabbed me by the throat about ten years later
when the big money I had been making
fell apart

it grabbed me because I had found things to do
which made the shame of my being
be quiet, but now the doing slowed
and the being part of human being
was lost

Circumstances come and go

But here's the truth:

I was wrong:

to disregard the feelings of the women I used for my pleasure

or ego

I was wrong:

To cheat when I was married or in a relationship

I was wrong:

To use people's money to gamble, without means to pay it back

I was wrong:

To allow my ex-wife to be unfair to my son, without taking action.

I forgave myself because I understood how desperate I felt, but I was wrong:

Because I wouldn't accept my explanation from someone else. I would have seen it as excuses.

Jesus forgives and loves us all, including the shamed me. But for me, honesty was and is the key that opens my soul wide to receive my full portion of love and grace. Jesus alone justifies me.

To Tell the Truth

Like your life depends on it,
tell the truth,
as your soul is revealed,
as you want to be known,
tell the truth,

It is a step, a small step,
but taken together,
the many steps
lead to freedom,
and freedom leads to authenticity,
and authenticity leads you to God,

and the fullness of His Grace!

The Demon Wins Until...

The drugs brought the doubt
and doubt is the demon's twin
then doubt doubles down on drugs
Then the Demon wins

But doubt has some powerful friends
and goes to wake up shame
then shame shamed the whole dang game
and still the Demon wins

Now bills come due
lies come due too
here comes deception
then misdirection and depression

and then time slows down
and pretty soon it's all
doubt and drugs and shame and lies
and drugs seem okay
because doubt and shame
have taken your brain
and it can turn bad...

or you escape
but it starts right over anyway

and on and on

and then one fine day

I said
One fine day!

I met a man named Jesus!

This is a different kind of power
This is filling-in-all-gaps power
This is every single question will be answered power
This is Trust in ME power

And Jesus has been with me ever since
He's Everything I Need and More!

Exodus

We lived under the lash for four hundred years
We saw the miracles.
Our exodus was miraculous
yet still we complained
about the manna, about being nomads
about almost everything…

so, we made a golden calf,
sent Moses to face the Almighty
and wandered, fussing for forty years,

til the next generation
cleansed of complaints
could find their way forward
to the promised land

Part II

When my parents died
I stumbled into my clear mind,
found my authentic voice
and mused that I could have realized this
long ago, when I first made my own way…
but It took forty years,

the death of a generation

for me to complete my exodus and fully see.

My Response to 'Exodus'

by Marcia Goranson

Wow. To be able to see with that much clarity. Even after so many years of wandering. Thanks be to God for preserving your life and bringing you here, to Ryan's Cathedral. Also, for keeping you here, in your Earth space, so that we may share in your perspective! I, myself have been a wanderer, searching for peace and relief from torment in my soul. I'm so thankful that our paths met and merged into this collaboration.

During the course of the soul work that I underwent, facilitated by you and your gift of insight, I found my long-lost self-respect and the realization that 'there was nothing wrong with me.' I was sexually abused as a child but the drive of my God-given sense of destiny would never let me settle or give in to a life and mindset of victimhood. Let's keep moving forward!

Come Home–a Song to the Split-off Child Within

by Tom Josephson

Come home, it's been too long
since you've been gone.
Come home to me on your own,
I will never leave you alone.

I don't remember anything other than
you gone.
Every word I ever spoke,
was a calling out to you,
everything I ever did,
I did for you too.

Don't let shame or failure
get in our way,
it was the split in our self
that took you, my true little boy self, away.

And I'm afraid I must tell you,
after all these futile years,

I can't heal it.
I can't fix it.
I can't make one solid self out of two.

But I'll never again leave you,
like a castaway of youth,
and though we may forever be two,
I'll always speak our truth.

It was then, upon accepting who and what I am,
that the noise that had been flooding my mind,
burst out like water through a dam.
And in the new quiet, the only thing left I could find

Were these words, inscribed in my soul:

"Come home to Me, the Lord, it's been too long
since you've been gone.
Come home to Me on your own,
I, the Lord, will never leave you alone."

I CAN HELP

What am I here for
if not to help
someone
step through their pain,
to help them clear
their confusion,
to name what they can't name,
to offer the truth
and the hope
that in due time
they can, and will,
be separate from their story,
that the unbearable of today,
will be just what's happened
some day.

The prices I've paid
have been steep,
but they were paid,
and now I'm here to help,

to talk about love and forgiveness,
to see the light turn on for a troubled soul,

to remind folks about Jesus,
respectfully, sincerely meet you
on your journey,
walk with you a while,
and remind you
what a precious gift
it all is,
and that somebody
cares.

IT'S GONNA BE OKAY

You don't know me,
unless you do,
and you might well say
"Who are you"?

Despite the prices I've paid,
I've stepped on through,
and made a way,
and learned a thing or two.

And the main thing I have to say is
it's gonna be okay,
you're gonna get there anyway.

And at the end of the long day
when there's nothing left to pay,
don't forget the blessings sent your way
and contemplate what I say.
Jesus came, it's gonna be okay.

A Change is Coming

The Holy Spirit is sweeping my soul
Into God's arms
carrying me
to a new day

A change surely is coming.

Lord, I pray You would teach me
to fully open my heart to You,
and anoint me, if it is Your will,
to call out to Your sheep who are lost
in these times,

What You ask is faith in God
but so many confuse
religiosity with You

But You gave me a different way to see
When You revealed Yourself directly to me,
You, in the Holy of Holies,
In God's place,
to me, outside
seeing You
where no man can go

me, a descendent of Holocaust Jews,
my mother's son,
a survivor who created herself
in triumphant denial,

As Mom absorbed "the pain, and fear, and hopelessness"
and created Victory
by how she lived,

so will I create the life I envision,
just as Mom did.
That is the change.
And that change is here.
Accepting Salvation in Christ,
In Whom I am born again was the rebirth

and my Victory converts my ancestors'
deaths in the ghettos and camps
into His Righteousness
and the Promise of my Savoir, Redeemer, and Deliverer.
Walking in faith as he asks, that is the change
that is the victory!
Thank you, Jesus!

I Could Blame Covid

I could blame Covid
for my being so out of shape,
but the truth is
I did this to myself,
one bite at a time.

Age is taking its toll on my body,
but my spirit is twenty-one!

Today is a day for laying down
with a cloud for a pillow,
a day to let my thoughts wander
out into the field,
to see them run and play,
to bask in the embrace of acceptance,
and step out from under the cloak of shame.

Today I feel good about who I am,
a child of the Living God,
perfected in His shed blood
and resurrection
Today my house
is the Lord's house,
for He is with me.

He is with me on the beach,
He is with me in the park,
He is with me in my very soul

He is Love
and I am loved,
He is Forgiveness,
and I am forgiven,
He is Righteousness
and I am righteous in His light,
He is a blessing to the world,
and I am greatly blessed!

PEACE AND QUIET

The night is still
and I have found the quiet
with an empty mind.
This silence is peaceful.
But something is emerging,
and I know what it is.

It is the presence of the Holy Spirit
filling the stillness.

Immersed as I now am
 It's easy to let go
of whatever I should let go,
whether thought, emotion or habit,
if it's negative,
if it's clutter
I will route it right out of my mind,
like rain down a gutter,

Just as you clean the house for company,
so too in this clear clean space of mind
comes the ultimate company,
the presence of the King

The Lord is here;
He is here,
Hallelujah!

PART THREE

RYAN'S CATHEDRAL

by Tom Josephson

A rupture in the darkness
chaos and colors
light exploding and pain
what, what, what
is this
this pain
dark and exploding fire?

Voices, voices in the distance
Mama mama....

Face.... face....step....step
Thank you!
Step...yes... Thank you!

My room...my room...my room
Thank you!
My brush
Thank you!

Jesus loves us
Thank you!

Clear the table
Thank you!

Take out the trash
Thank you!
Taking out the trash
Thank you!

The large blue box
This is the small one
Thank you!

This is where we pray
Thank you!
Pray for brother, thank you, Lord!
Pray for sister
Thank you, Lord!
Pray for Ms. Anna
Thank you, Lord!

Taking my lunch
Thank you!
Dishes in the sink
Thank you!
A small green plate
Thank you!

Excuse me, Mr. Tom
Thank you!
Mr. Tom,
Thank you!

This is where we pray
Thank you, Lord!

Praying for sister
Thank you!
Praying for Brother
Thank you
Praying for Ms. Anna
Thank you!

Thank you, Lord!
Do you see?
Do you see?
Thank you, Lord!

Turning off the TV
Thank You, Lord!
Turning off the lights
Thank you!
Mr. Tom's not finished
Thank you!
A small green plate
Thank you!

This is holy.
Thank you, Lord!
Holy, yes, Lord!
Thank you, Lord!

You are perfect
Thank you!
Perfect yes,
Thank you!
Perfect
Thank you, Lord!
This is where we pray
Thank you!
Praying for Sister
Thank you, Lord!
Praying for Brother
Thank you, Lord!
Praying for Ms. Anna
Thank you, Lord!
Placing his hand on Mr. Tom
Thank you!

Praying for Mr. Tom
Thank you, Lord!

Thank you, Lord!
Taking my lunch
Thank you!
Thank you, Lord!

Taking out the trash
Thank you!
Getting the clothes from your room
Thank you!
Mr. Tom's foot isn't swollen
Thank you, Lord!
Thank you!
Mr. Tom's foot
I know Mr. Tom... I know

Thank you!

Part Two

Ryan's touch was certain on my shoulder,
nothing uncertain,
not too firm, not too light,
just a connection,
from the Lord!
And now my foot looks like it once did,
Thank you, Lord.

He paces.
His fingers wag like cat whiskers.
He is the canary in the SOUL MINE!

No soul can enter or leave
he doesn't see,
even far away...
He ascends the steps to his room,

saying "thank you!"
He goes to
his UPPER ROOM.

From aloft
he descends to pace,
and protect the space
we cannot see.

A mighty warrior!
Who, in the midst of chaos
creates an ethos
of rituals which we do see!

Here we are,
in a world resplendent
with grace
where the table is set
by the Holy Spirit,
and the food is delivered
by Ryan, the one who gives thanks
for everything in this life!
Thank you, Lord!

Thank you!

A Response to 'Ryan's Cathedral'

by Marcia Goranson

We knew when we spotted the land that one day it should be ours to steward. We knew also as the house went up it was a special place. As the walls and floors fit together, we knew it would be a healing space. The comfort that lives here is God-breathed, filling our lives with peace. To us it's home, to others a retreat.

The prophet Tom, came and stayed and lived and breathed in the healing place, watched over and tended to by Ryan, the guardian of the grace.

While here, the prophet healed and changed his point of view, growing closer to Messiah and His loving embrace.

The Prophet's words hold volumes of truth, inspired by the Spirit, the living channel of hope, help and conviction. Take heed and listen to the message he conveys. It contains life and hope and praise for the one who constructed Ryan's Cathedral, a vibrant yet humble space, meant for those who need a healing grace.

Inspecting Ryan's Cathedral

I have come to inspect this place,
this cathedral in space,
to find out of what it is made.

I have seen the spiritual fruits
this powerful place has produced,
and I wonder what price has been paid?

I stayed here.
I learned here.
And this is the scene that was played:

Ryan is the one who sees
the things we can't see.
I've seen this in the time I stayed.

Ryan stays lit in the Spirit,
not just for a moment or in fits,
but day after day after day!

His tools are service and loyalty.
His bricks are gratitude.
His foundation is faith.
His mortar is love.

His rituals, his pacing,
are what you do
when the light is so bright,
that he, living in that light,
needs them to function in this world.

Others may see disabilities.
But I see grace.
I see he is close to God.

Ryan builds his cathedral daily,
with the love and support of his family,
people who walk in their faith.

I have finished my inspection,
and here is my conclusion.
These fruits are no accident.
They are Spirit-filled infusions!
And miracles pay the Holy rent!

Ryan Rides a Horse

He sits straight and stiff-backed on his steed,
his legs are powerfully poised,
perfectly placed for control, for assurance,
that he is in full command,
and the horse is quiet, at the ready

And as Ryan rides,
as he walks, then trots, he displays
the rhythm of royalty.

It is a flawless cadence, their trotting
across the dirt floor of the arena,

and I see a mighty army of angels
lining up, mounted, and ready
for Ryan to lead the charge
that welcomes the Lord in the air

His presence on that horse heralds
the Almighty, to let loose the triumphant return
of the King, slashing out of the sky!

And Ryan's army charges up to join the Lord
in the day the Truth is revealed.

THE WARRIOR LOST IN THE WOODS

We met in the woods
next to the park,
hidden near a bridge over the spillway.

He stopped his bike
as our paths crossed,
and we talked.

An hour passed,
we were lost in another world
of connection.

He had fought in the jungles of Vietnam,
and was comfortable
hidden in these woods;

but not "in the world,"
not among the people,
for whom he fought,

nor the offices of professionals,
or the company of family
who told him he needed to mingle,

and was plagued by judgment,
his own self-judgment
that he had failed at peace.

He was a warrior
who lived with the two-fold pain in his heart
of battle and alienation.

He was a warrior
who cried when I said it was okay
to take care of himself.

He was a warrior
who prevailed in the jungle,
but was lost in the woods.

LIONEL AND OSCAR

L ionel and I spoke for two or three hours this past August. He told me the following:

Some fifty-five years ago, during his father, Oscar's funeral service, Lionel looked up at the balcony of the church. He was reminded of his father's tailor shop on 146th in Harlem...

Lionel s father, Oscar, had returned from World War II and opened this neighborhood shop. He became a humble resource for the disaffected. If you needed to show employment for your PO, Oscar would sign off...."and don't forget to wear a coat and tie when you come to the Lord's house," he would remind one and all

He would give clothes left behind or donated in his shop to those who might need to look their best for a judge or a job, or to pay respects, with his usual refrain..."make sure you dress correct when you come to the Lord's house..."

And Oscar would remind his son, "Lionel, don't you forget to dress right for the Lord"

Oscar didn't have much to give. But gave what he could...

As the pastor eulogized Oscar, Lionel saw in the church balcony some of those same convicts and gangsters and dealers and junkies and others of the marginalized whose lives his father had touched and blessed...

Saw they were dressed "correct," many in the very suits and jackets his father had given them from his shop ....

They had dressed correct for the Lord's house, as Oscar used to say, for the send-off of this good man, Oscar Phillips. His credo fulfilled, Oscar Phillips was escorted correct on his journey home....and his son, Lionel, scanned the balcony and smiled through his tears.

Lionel was insistent that I get this little piece right. He reviewed it and called me back the next day with corrections. I re-emailed it to him substantially in this form. Lionel died about a month afterwards.

A HERO TURNS NINETY

A simple man,
a man of the earth
farmed in heat and cold,
farmed through dry Oklahoma summers,
picked cotton,
cut watermelons for his daughters
alongside him in the fields,
worked cows and raised chickens,
plowed the ground
for food,
went to church,

and then went to war.

Put on a uniform
proudly and without complaint,
faced Nazis like he faced the wind
coming out of the western plains
back home,
something that just needed to be done.

No whining,
no whimpering,
as shells blew his friends

to smithereens
on Omaha beach,
body parts mixing with sand,
exploding as he scurried,
screams and howitzers
howling,
a glimpse of hell on earth,
blowing out his eardrums,
but not the stench of burning flesh.

Deployed then to the frozen Ardennes,
frostbitten and unbathed,
day after day,
week after week,
dug in without a change of clothes,
months of mortal combat,
as tens of thousands of American soldiers died,
farmers, truck drivers
steel workers.

A noble name we give this frostbitten winter,
"Battle of the Bulge" we call it,
but labels can't capture the horror,
the reality of so many dead,
of killing,
of facing death daily,
no rest, no warmth, no safety,
no peace.

And the fighting stopped.

And the sounds of war went mute,
except for the nightmares
and explosions at night in dreams
he suffers alone,
the shock of the farm,
standing in wait,
life, waiting for him.

And he stepped back into that role
without complaint.
His wife and the child
who didn't know her daddy,
and new daughters and son,
lived the dream so many
fought and died to create.

Ran a rural mail route,
and farmed long days,
raised his children,
went to church,

and without complaint,
this quiet and good man turns ninety,
in his spare home,
neat and orderly,
medals and ribbons hanging on a wall
quietly,
inconspicuously like the man.

With no chest beating,
with no despair
or self-indulgence,
the medals still and quiet,
like an empty battlefield,
tokens of horror,
survival and sacrifice,
this dignified, quiet man
has graced the earth ninety years,
has served his country,
loved and supported his family,
honored his faith,
fought wars in sleep every night,
enjoyed simple things,
good things,
without complaint.

But for him,
and others who served,
fought and died,
my people, the Jews, would be vanished off the earth.

I say a hero has lived among us,
though he will deny it;
but words are not his calling,
I am the mouthpiece on this occasion,

an occasion of family and faith,
love and remembrance,

honor and gratitude:
A tip of the cap to you, Bob Spitzer,
a hero from Sayre, Oklahoma,
turning ninety,
written nobly, justly, into the history of the world
forever.

Happy birthday to you Bob Spitzer,
a good man, a decent man,
a man I am proud to know,
a hero who has turned ninety today,
happy birthday, thank you
and God bless!

In Memory of Jack Weisblack

Jack Weisblack died yesterday.
He passed out of this world
leaving it better than he got,
and worse off for his leaving

My cousin died yesterday, my teacher, my mentor
in many things,
my conduit, my connection…

Jack was seventeen when the Nazis came to Poland.

Being useful, Jack survived
the decimation of Lodz (pronounced Ludge) Ghetto,
Lodz, a city of 200,000 Jews reduced to rubble, stepping over
dying children crying for food,
crying for their mothers, crying for mercy,
stepping past the cries, helpless, in search of bread while his own
family disappeared and died,
or perished, as my grandmother used to say,
gassed in Auschwitz or starved in the ghetto,
seventy-five souls, everyone he knew,
everyone he loved,
Jack witnessed their slaughter.

at the hands of the Third Reich,
and survived.

And when Lodz Ghetto was "liquidated"
Jack was rounded up and shipped like cattle to Hell.

To Auschwitz he went.

Jack smelled the fumes
billowing out of the ovens in Auschwitz,
saw the ashes fall like snow,
perhaps the fumes and ashes of his dead brethren,
but then again, as Jack knew,
all are brethren in the ovens,
all are brethren in God's eyes,
but these Nazis were men of Hell not God,
and he survived.

Being useful, Jack survived, and saw
the beating to death of two of my cousins
asking for soup to soothe their starving bones
in Auschwitz yard.

And Jack knew
Sonder commandos in Auschwitz,
Jews in charge of disposing of the ashes and carcasses of the dead,
knew they were carted like trash,
human beings, our family,
carted like filthy trash,
and incinerated, or dumped in slimy heaps,

in great stinking pits, limbs slick with death, witnessed these wit-
nesses of death in Hell, and Jack survived.

The man I knew in the New York of my youth,
my cousin, sounded foreign, loved hockey,
loved his Cadillac, loved the business he built
with his hands, being always useful,
lived his life greatly, loved his son, loved his wife,
my cousin Phyllis,
loved life, had a smile for everyone, and a kind word, encouraged
everyone he met, radiated warmth
to me growing up in New York,
and to everyone.

And when I was ready Jack opened his heart
and showed me Hell,
poured out his story not for himself, but for those whose destruc-
tion he witnessed and survived.

Always useful, Jack survived Hell with a kind word, with encouragement for all,
with a smile for the world,
he survived.

But more than that
Jack Weisblack lived
in happiness!

Jack Weisblack died yesterday, my mentor,
my conduit not just to the horror, but to life,

life with a kind word, a smile, encouragement to all.
Jack Weisblack, my cousin, lived well
and died yesterday.

Response to 'In Memory of Jack Weisblack'

by Marcia Goranson

What a testimony of the human spirit. He refused to live and think like a victim. He was able to be honest regarding the suffering he had endured and seen firsthand. He processed through the horror somehow and wouldn't allow the Evil to win.

What a fine man and a true hero. So much like Sophie. They were spared and survived, determined to make the most of the lives they found and made in a new country.

Give us this resolve Lord.

ONE DAY THIS WILL ALL BE OVER

One day this will all be over for me
and for you, reading this
one day I will pray for one more Spring.
with its long days of Sunlight,
I will pray to know my granddaughter,
and for her to know me,
and for some measure of acceptance
which I pray can take place
before I leave forever
a broken father.

One day I will beseech the Almighty
to cleanse me for my journey into forever,
so, I can see again
the blessings bestowed freely,
to see the morning sun glimmer between the trees
and reflect on a pond
as I walk my dog
in perfect union,
to play baseball with my son all those glorious days,
to be the legacy bearer of my Holocausted family

And for my great friends,
Marcia and Roger, Anna and Brenda and Clinton
and the Mighty Spirit in Ryan
and for my life partner, Loretta....
and the final blessing, to feel love,
however broken, as I leave this life,

What Would You Have Me Do?

Ups and downs,
near death, ICU, Covid, cancer,
so many changes
why did You reveal Yourself to me?

Trials, tribulations, faith, doubt,
so many mistakes
my son is ashamed,
why did You reveal Yourself to me?

Alienated, diagnosed, medicated
placated, beaten and broke
nothing to show for it all
why did You reveal Yourself to me?

Yes, there will be more to face,
the fingers pointed,
the disgrace on my name,
yet You keep coming for me.

Have I been anointed by the Spirit?
Is that the power I seek when I write?
Is the illumination the light of God the Father?

Are the words His?

Is my gift

Him revealed through my searching for the right thing to say?

Is the alignment between what I mean and what you hear

Is that part of being anointed in the Spirit?

What would You have me do?

Is accepting the voice You gave

and protected

Your plan for me?

Is reaching out to be a guide

to the broken, to the lost, to the hurting

to bring comfort and truth,

in Sophie's Voice,

and in my own voice,

is the discernment I need His?

Are You Him?

Yes, I will help. Is that why I was saved?

And yes, I will yield my will to Yours,

You are my Savior,

You are my Redeemer

You are sent on behalf of Him

Who created everything

and …. Yes, I accept Your anointing.

LIMITLESS LOVE

Next month, God willing I will turn seventy-three,
and there can be no denying
my time here is waiting to meet my end

and the question it will ask is
"have you used up your love?"

And my question to myself
Is that very question,
"Have I given it all?
Have I told the Lord
How much I love the life
He freely gave?
Have I prayed enough?

Have I given fully to those I love?
Have I let the trees know?
Have I let the sea birds
and mountain birds know?
Have I spoken praise enough
of the gifts of this world?
 Have I celebrated enough?
Have I spoken love to my friends?
Have I given everything I possibly could

to my son,
and his family?
Have I honored it all?
Have I showed love
to Loretta, that will shine
no matter what?

My love is not much
In Your Holy Light and Love,
Yet You love me infinitely

How Great Thou Art!

You Don't Have to Understand

I was explaining where it was
that Jesus revealed Himself.

I stood up, facing a window,
as I had stood
in front of the Holy of Holies;
but this time as a Christian,
this time it was as though
the curtain was already rent;
this time the space was open
and Jesus was deep inside

Suddenly, I couldn't control my body,
my knees buckled,
I braced myself on this solid sturdy table
and slid, trembling and sobbing
into the chair

I couldn't hold my head up,
I couldn't speak.
Finally, I asked for help
and went to lay down.
I was overcome by the Presence.

Lord, guide me, give me wisdom
give me discernment.
Help me say the right things.
I am not worthy.
Yet you touched me.

"Open your mouth and let the words come.
You are anointed.
You are not speaking for yourself
and you don't have to understand.
You belong to ME.
Suspend your mind,
get yourself out of the way
and trust The Holy Spirit.
Let My Father's Will speak,
In My name, in My Holy name,
through the Holy Spirit.
This is no longer about you."

Yes Lord.
Thank you, Jesus.

THE RIGHT PATH

There is a vision
Then a path
Then the way
Then the stand
Then the truth
Then the walk
Then righteousness
Then forgiveness
Then emptiness
Then authenticity

Then God

Then leaning in
Then walking in Faith
Then service to others

Then Jesus

Then healing
Then love
Then the Holy Spirit
and Paradise

The Bridge

A bridge is a structure that spans and provides passage over a road, railway, river or some other obstacle. In terms of our book, *Sophie's Voice*, I am writing these paragraphs to construct a bridge between Tom's creative writing and my creative writing. It is sort of like an interlude or an intermission.

In another point of view, I would describe my relationship with Tom as, yes, my bridge over and into a huge obstacle in my life. The resolution of my trauma. Along with my husband's support, he has literally coached me to the living end of my road to recovery from childhood sexual trauma and the extra effects of the silent invalidation of my pain. My writing here depicts the intensity of the past four to five months of processing and all that it entails. It's been a very tough but remarkable soul workout. Tom helped me sort through the haze and find the real culprits of my bondage. Fear and shame.

I'm so looking forward to the day of being completely whole, spirit soul and body. On that day I'll see the face of Jesus. Until then, I'll be working to maintain my emotional and mental health and Tom and I and my husband want to extend our hands to others who are in the same confusing haze that is the trauma trap.

PART FOUR

Marcia's Process

The Poet's Back in Town
by Tom Josephson

The poet's back in town
singing the songs we would,
dancing the dance we would,
living the life we would
if we could,

The poet's back in town
going mute for us,
feeling pain for us,
emptying his soul and dying for us
like we would
if we could

soon the poet will leave town,
we will settle into a dream again,
talk of the same old days again,
feel those same old blues again

and wait for the poet's return again
living the life we would if we could.

SYMPHONY

There's a symphony in me.

The master arrangement is written by His holy hands.

I'm the composer, He allows me to steward His masterpiece,

To translate what I hear and feel and sense from the pen to the paper and beyond.

The conductor is the Spirit, weaving it together as only He can.

I hear words as others hear notes.

My melody lines use grammar, verbs and adjectives.

The allegro reaches a crescendo, as the harmony comes in to make it complete.

So, let it play…inspire, soothe, encourage and motivate.

Take it in and let the living thing become part of you…

Revealing a side of the Master's creative genius that He gives and gifts to us

To enjoy and love…just as He does.

SPARKLE

On a dark but moonlit night, the snow was shimmering and cold. It was what we knew though–what we were born to. We thought nothing of the freezing temperature.

There was a short but steep hill in the neighbor's yard and we had a fast sled. The ride was quick and the snow crunched under the weight.

At the bottom, we stood up as quickly as our layers of clothes would allow. We had red noses and cheeks but our fingers and toes were still warm. 'Let's go again' was our cry.

When we finally tired, she said to me 'There is such a sparkle in your eyes.' 'You're so special!'

She had always treated me that way. She let me know that I was valuable and precious. 'If I had a daughter, I'd want her to be just like you.' Of course, she meant what she said. I was a treasure to her and she didn't hesitate to say it.

How could it be then that my greatest betrayal would take place in her house and at the hands of her son!

My childhood as well as my self-image and even my true personhood was devastated…stolen and brutally brought down in shame when he perpetuated ungodly and perverted acts upon my body and soul.

He shattered and violently robbed me of my innocence. My child's mind was opened to the knowledge of good and evil. Adult awareness of sex acts was no longer foreign to me. I was forced fully awake to my own sexuality before I was ten years old.

Did I continue to love her, the perpetrator's mother? Yes. In my confused but now open immaturity, I felt that I was responsible for protecting her from the truth about her son and the evil things he had done to me. His shame became mine to conceal. From everyone.

Thus, my life was set upon a course of victimhood that threatened to become fixed in my psyche over the course of my lifetime. Victimhood attempted to bury the person that I was born to be.

It became easier and easier to lie and just present what I knew everyone wanted to see. That I was fine. The same little girl I had always been. So, in effect, I shut down and froze my emotions. No one could ever know or even suspect what had happened…that I was going to become what had been done to me.

My Sparkle had been shredded and stolen. My job was to perfect a replica of my true self to everyone. No one else could ever know how shameful and horrible I was. Would my true Sparkle ever be restored? I never believed it was possible.

HE LOVES ME MORE

'I think the Lord wants me to do something.' I said to her. I knew there was a risk...breaking the silence of my heart and revealing my internal struggle to her. There was no resistance or wisdom or prayer from her that day...only a re-direction.

I was born in the Baby Boomer generation...in Midwest America. Hard work and conservative lifestyles were the norm.

Both of my parents were born during the Great Depression of the 1930s...and they were in the fight to break out of the poverty that they had each come from. That was their focus. Dreams were just delusions.

They met, married, and had their first child while they were very young. Brimming with their own unresolved familial trauma, each one had their own way of bypassing and ignoring their own pain and carrying on like nothing had ever happened to them.

My mother's ideal was to continue the domestic fantasy of the 1950s. Her job as the mother of a daughter was to attempt to conform me into a model of a society that was quickly fleeting. In essence, I was raised and trained to settle for a safe, small life...compliant to the accepted norms of a fading facade.

In the midst of their struggle however, a most outstanding gift was given to me. I was taught who Jesus Christ is and why I needed Him.

Outside of the saving knowledge though, as far as daily living and plans for the future were concerned, there was no encouragement or help in finding my God-given gifts and to strive to develop them—for His glory and for a fulfilling life for me.

The majority of their time and energy was spent on rising above and staying above the poverty line. Then, secondarily was the effort it took to live and present according to expectations of all kinds. Expectations both spoken and unspoken.

There was no sharing of hopes and dreams…no encouragement to find a deeper walk with Christ.

Instead, I was taught by example and the modeling of unspoken rules regarding how to live according to and in line with an invisible script. Rules such as…keep your emotions hidden, never tell the whole truth, don't expect much more from life other than following in our footsteps. Stay inside the safe, confining parameters…especially if you are female.

Deaden and deny any supernatural spark of hope and destiny. Freedom to become the person you were born to be was not part of the plan. It was not written into the script.

Become a good employee but don't aspire to much higher. Defeat poverty but don't allow yourself to dream or think like an overcomer. Never lift your eyes or your thoughts above your current horizon.

A good job, a husband and children. A home with a mortgage was considered success. Never think about stretching beyond…who do you think you are after all?

Then–I was given another gift, while still a very young child. A book. A large hard back Children's Bible. It became my open door to a much broader view of life and history and the hope of a future made by God's design. Even for people who had huge problems and didn't always follow the rules.

As I sat in a warm spot on the floor of my parents' basement I opened and devoured the pictures and stories in that Bible. I realized even then that the pages were alive with the presence of Jesus Christ Himself. He revealed Himself to me. He was gentle and kind. He gave me a heart to love Him. I knew His voice from then on.

On the basement floor with that big book in my lap, I developed an awareness of the Lord's heart. A seed of destiny began incubating in me during those moments in my early childhood.

The Godly spark of destiny was in my DNA. Its call was in my blood, coming all the way from my ancient great grandfather William Warren, who fought with William the Conqueror and helped him gain the throne of England.

To my other great grandfather, Richard Warren, who made the voyage to the New World on the Mayflower.

To my great-great-grandmother, Catherine Almira Warren Jacobs, who was born in New York. She pioneered west and kept going even after her father drowned in Lake Champlain, when she was eleven.

She met and married my great, great grandfather, George Jacobs, a German immigrant who spoke very little English. Together they settled and homesteaded in Iowa and broke virgin ground.

Their pioneer spirit and drive for a better life has always reverberated in me. It's in my genetic make-up. I wondered many times as a child what my mission was and where will it take me?

Then, at twelve years of age, I made a public pledge of my heart to Jesus Christ one evening during an altar call. He had been real to me but I had never heard anyone give an invitation to dedicate my life to Him. I responded in gratitude and the faith of a child.

By that time, I had been suffering with the effects and consequences of childhood sexual trauma. Silently. Locked up by my family system.

Incest. The rape of my childhood and my personhood.

In my child's mind, I was tragically and devastatingly mistaken when I believed that I was corrupted. That I was at fault, that there was something terribly wrong with me. All of those false beliefs went underground in me.

The crushing repercussions of the perpetrator's crimes forced me to become an absolute pretender, hiding and silently protecting him and his enablers. I believed it was my fault. That lie made me believe that it was my job to join in the cover up of his crimes. It twisted my mind and his shame covered my sense of self. The shredding of my soul was done on purpose. To extinguish the Holy spark of eternal life and mission in me and to violently rob me, the innocent one of any semblance of a healthy life.

Shame and guilt, searing and unresolved, sought to smother my God-given desires and motivation that had been invested in me. I struggled mightily to keep the facade of being 'me', of being 'fine,' all through my teenage years and young adulthood. My full-time profession became 'the maintainer of the unholy family charade.' I was burning with anger and desperation but there was no respite, no hero for me. For many years.

But... the underlying force of the truth of who I was and who I belonged to would not let my heart stop and fully believe that I was going to become what had been done to me.

The truth was residing in my heart and soul, buried deeply but not extinguished. No matter how polluted my outward life became and no matter how loudly the lies screamed at me—keeping me powerless and endlessly adrift.

Pride, ignorance, guilt, shame, greed, envy and apathy, ... none of them could kill the righteous life that belonged to Christ.

In my late teens I miraculously survived stage three melanoma. The prognosis was death by age twenty-five. That was in 1979.

I reacted badly to the declaration of death over my life. Filled with fear and confusion—I ran...hard and fast...for four years. But—the truth was—I belonged to Christ. I had let go of Him...believing that I had disqualified myself from His love. Everywhere I ran though during those lost years, the Good Shepherd was already there to meet me. Gently calling me back to His side…nudging me gently and lovingly away from danger and even suicide.

After fumbling and floundering around…I finally ran out of strength to run. The battle in my soul between what I falsely believed about myself and the truth about who I could be waged relentlessly, until my twenty-third year.

My spiritual father called me to meet him in his front room one evening, March 1, 1983, four years to the day that I had received the news that I had cancer. He once again explained the details of the healing of the melanoma that had occurred four years prior. This time I heard it and I knew that I was going to live. For a long time.

The Good Shepherd was there along with the Helper, the Holy Spirit. His Holy presence filled that room and His goodness and mercy cradled my heart…I said yes to Him again and He took my weary soul in His arms. My confusion and angry resistance met His loving, merciful embrace and dissipated like a fog lifting…I gave Him my child's wounded heart and I fell completely in love with Him…for always.

I knew beyond any doubt and without reservation that He loved ME more…and it changed everything for me. His love surrounded me like a fortress and I found a place inside it to find rest for my sick and weary soul…in His Everlasting Arms.

I knew that I loved Him more than my messy life. What I didn't realize that night though, was that the pain and shame of the unprocessed sexual trauma was still buried too deeply. It was too painful and hideous to even approach. I was only beginning my walk with Him. I no longer felt disqualified from receiving His love but the poison of the buried secrets of shame would take a long, long time to work themselves to the top level of my pain tolerance.

Looking back, my heart wishes that I had begun the process of healing so much sooner. The silent, suffocating chaos of the effects of childhood sexual trauma and the non-supportive, invalidating system that was keeping me spinning in the same cycle of victimhood was a powerful mental and emotional lockdown device. There was no help, but I didn't realize that I belonged to Jesus Christ and that He hears and answers the cries of the heart of His children. I was bound illegally. I belonged to Him. He would not let it stand.

Soon after that night of new found freedom, I left behind my confining comfort zone and began a new life. I began traveling a long road. But this time I knew I wasn't alone.

Yes…it was a narrow path but it was bounded now by His Shepherd's staff…keeping me safe and moving forward… slowly but steadily…through the years….with a goal in sight now…my destiny, the development of my missionary heart and where it would lead me.

He helped me learn how to remain constant in the middle of the struggle of daily living. Even as I continued to bear the mix of shame, unspoken and unprocessed pain.

The weight was becoming too cumbersome and heavy but because I was young, I was able to carry it all…then…

Marriage required a new level of functionality. Having children brought a new weight of accountability.

A move with family found me void of coping ability…
pretense will no longer cover and carry the pain. Dysfunction
threatened to blow my life apart.

The Good Shepherd nudged me into a place reserved just
for me. His holy hands made a cleft for me…inside Himself.
A real place…a safe place to begin and maintain the process
of becoming honest and truly healing. The work of digging
into buried but living shame and guilt and lies had begun…at
mid-life.

Its excruciating to begin to break the family code of silence
and say the words–-'I suffered molestation…incest…at the
hands of my blood relative…a grown man…using and abusing
and perverting his cousin…me…at seven years of age.

It was extremely difficult to release the traumatic events that
had been locked in the vault in the bottom of my soul for so
long…but…He never left me or turned away. He loved ME
more.

I continued to process the horror of my underground, double
life at a precariously slow pace it seemed…but where else could
I go to find life…authentic life and the freedom to become my
true self.

His shepherd's staff never ceased to lovingly urge me forward
through those years. The realization and the self-awareness
that I gained… along with the deconstruction of the false life
I maintained and endured for everyone else's sake…made the
discomfort of swimming upward out of the scummy swamp of
terror and shame worth all the work.

The Helper continued chipping away at the block of marble that was my human condition. He knew that the masterpiece was somewhere in the marble...revealing itself more and more as I continued unlearning all the falsehoods that I had believed...mainly about myself.

Then I was reminded by a friend of the ancestral DNA and the pioneer blood that makes up a large percentage of my heritage.

The pioneer drive had been dormant for two generations before I was born...the family was settled and had turned their attention to being productive and living in the fruit of what had been sown by the lives of their forefathers and mothers.

That settling had caused an allowance, an enabling of a seed of evil that had penetrated the family line. The greatness that lay in store for the family was invaded and there was a diabolical attempt to thwart and destroy the goodness from the inside out.

The demonic perversion of familial sexual trauma landed hard on my generation. It endangered the sanctity and prosperity intended for us.

As a victim, the protection of the heinousness became an impenetrable barrier to health and happiness in my life.

Then...in the latter stages of my recovery I became increasingly conscious of who I was. I was a descendant of over-comers. Brave ones who set out in faith and lived out their trust in the Creator...the one who had bestowed them with the will to push through the hard, seemingly indestructible obstacles in the course of life. Because of the hope and promise of greatness in store for them, they endured and persevered and followed peace, happiness, wholeness, and love.

Then, my friend, the older brother I'd never had, became the greatest source of feedback and encouragement. His insight broke through the barrier of false beliefs and I was unafraid to tell the truth for the first time in my life. All of it. The ugly, putrid truth. With his and my husband's support, the power of the truth broke the hold of shame and fear that had paralyzed me since I was a child.

My encourager is who I had needed all along—a flesh and blood brother whose gifts of perception and exhortation had been forged in his own battles in the fiery furnace of terror and shame.

His viewpoint and intuitive skill put me through an emotional boot camp…an intensive few weeks that enabled and readied me to face the final and most soul deadening weapon that the enemy of my soul could muster against me…Shame.

The exhorter led me to face the wide-open chasm of terror… he gave me the tools and support to identify it, call it out and finally forsake it.

The living, foaming and stagnant, wet wool blanket of shame had covered and silenced my true self and voice. It took more than fifty years to recover from the robbery of my childhood and true sense of self. My self-worth and self-esteem had lain at the bottom of the deepest abyss of my soul…infected with impotence and loathing but never destroyed.

My God-given missionary heart…my heritage…my destiny…lay there also…crying and groaning for revitalization and release. The insidious device almost completely convinced me to disqualify myself from a Godly destiny because I was becoming what had been done to me.

Its power was strong but its strength lay only in deception… it was all a lie! A multitude of lies!

Once my heart's eyes were opened to the truth––that the name of Jesus was higher and more powerful than shame, pain or sexual perversion…the wicked ungodliness masquerading as my true self disintegrated.

While there–standing in the light of the truth–I saw my outrage as well…formerly buried with all my unresolved issues.

I stood up as my true self–as Brave Heart and I grabbed that outrage and swung it like the Shepherd's staff and smashed the shame into a fine dust and it blew away as the Helper breathed on me…the breath of new life! The life of an overcomer…a thriver…no longer a victim dripping with shame and I grabbed hold of the life I was born to live and the person who was born to live it!

The little girl reading that Children's Bible in a warm spot on the floor of my parent's basement was alive again! Fully alive! Full of self-respect and self-esteem. I can now truly love my neighbor as I do myself and love Him, Jesus Christ the Good Shepherd, first….love Him more because He first loved ME more.

My friend, allow Him to lead you into the fullness of who you were created to be…no matter where you've been or what you've done. Freedom and peace wait for you. Step into stride with Him. His blood covers it all…our mistakes, our past, our future. There is no greater power of solution in the Universe. The name of Jesus and the unending truth of His Resurrection life is available for any need, any life, any time. It's not too late. He will never leave you or fail you. He loves YOU more!

A Girl, a Hope, and Bible

A Response to He Loves Me More by Tom Josephson

There wasn't much to feel good about
in the family into which
she was born.
a girl.

Her mother made sure she felt
her disappointment
in so many downcast looks,
so many, so many ways
to feel less than,

so many days,
so many dark days,
lay ahead for the girl
with the far away eyes,
as she learned her place,
which was no place,

a little girl with no face
and no place,
but she was part of the family,

so, they took her with them
to Church.

Yes, they got that part right.
Then the little one got her own picture book,
her own Holy Book,
and soon found a warm nook,
in the basement.

So, she had this space of freedom
and grace,

and Lord knows she needed it,
because before too long that little girl's life
was decimated.

But the light, the warmth, the glow
of Jesus and His love
brought her all the way,
all the long way
through the darkness
of incest,
silence and shame
to the Cross.

And though that family didn't know
how to stay in the Holy Light,
they knew to take that girl to church.

Her Mama knew what life held for her baby girl,
and, powerless as Mom felt

she gave that little girl,
life and a lifeline.

That girl met Jesus in that beautiful basement space.
She found her own face.
Hear her roar!

PARABLE OF THE ROSE SEED

Tom Josephson

For the purposes of this parable, we will consider rose seeds. Feel free to insert your own flower of choice.

You buy a package of seeds. On the cover is a picture of a beautiful red rose. When you open the package there are seeds, not a fully grown rose, but seeds, which should grow into roses.

Suppose we put five seeds in five pots and pack the pots with soil from the same bag, and put them all on a shelf near a window. We water them each day, but we notice, after a couple of weeks, four of the flowers have grown up to look like roses, but the fifth is small, bent and brown.

We quickly realize the fifth flower pot was blocked from sunlight most of the day. So, we remove whatever it was that was blocking the sunlight. Within a few days the fifth seedling begins to look better, but still not the same as the others.

We can therefore deduce it was not anything intrinsic in the seed that was unhealthy, it was simply a matter of inattention on the part of the caretaker that caused the seed to become unhealthy. We know that seed was not responsible; but the seed, before it becomes aware of the big picture, believes things about its character.

From the point of view of the seed, who cannot not see from outside its frame of reference to the perspective of the human who was responsible to nurture that seed, what would that seed think about itself when it saw all the other seedlings?

Wouldn't that poorly nurtured seed think many of the same things you who may have been abused or traumatized think?

Things like:

"There's something wrong with me"

"I'm a failure"

"I'm worthless"

Of course, that neglected seed would think those or similar thoughts, even when she became physically healthy and looked just like the other four roses. But we know, the thoughts would be wrong, understandable, but not accurate, not true.

As children, we are not responsible to nurture ourselves, any more than the rose seeds. I assure you, if you have those or similar thoughts, you were not watered, not nurtured properly! What I want you to know, if nothing, else, know this:

"There's nothing wrong with you!"

Never was, but you couldn't know that yet.

So, take heart, just because your understanding was limited, by your age, and your natural and normal dependence on others for getting your survival needs met, doesn't mean there's anything wrong. You can learn what the distortions in your thinking are, and it's perfectly okay, in fact, it's healthy, to address it, perhaps with a little help from friends, or a coach!

Once you understand that you didn't see accurately from the perspective of the big picture, because that understanding was blocked from you due to your dependency, and the capacity of understanding related to your stage of cognitive development (how much of this analysis would a five year old understand, regardless of her IQ), much as the sun was blocked from that rose seed, and that wasn't your fault, any more than it was the rose seed's "fault" to not attend to its own nurturing, then you can begin to take responsibility for unlearning the inaccuracies, and making your adult mind up about what you really believe.

In addition to the content of what you decide, the act of making changes for yourself starts a positive feedback loop of self-empowerment. You begin to feel better about yourself by the fact that you've seen the truth of how you got bent and bowed in the first place, and that there really is nothing wrong with you!

SCAPEGOAT

As it roamed the Earth…evil sought out those it could devour. The diabolical entity manufactured a vicious scheme to take advantage of the weaknesses in dysfunctional individuals and families. It preyed upon the guilt, shame and rock-hard pride of traumatized victims of abuse and pernicious neglect. In utter ignorance of the truth, those who were violated turned their own unresolved woundedness onto the innocent souls and psyches of their own children…their innocent ones. Given to them to cherish and nurture. Instead of valuing and inspiring…they instead, unwittingly or even purposely—firmly cast the burden of their own unresolved pain and agony onto and into the inward parts of their precious ones.

One unsuspecting child in each generation was chosen to bear the gross and unrelenting multi-generational cargo. The emotionally disturbed parents' own flesh and blood was designated to be the bearer of particularly tragic, searing and soul deadening toxic shame…which is fueled by fear so deadly that it paralyzed and fogged their child's heart and mind.

This innocent one, the family scapegoat, is weighted down with packs and truckloads of lies along with the history of multigenerational agony, neglect, blame and guilt.

The emotionally scarred and blinded parents transferred every rock and boulder of unprocessed, festering trauma from their souls into the packs and crates loaded onto the scapegoat child to bear.

They fed their own emotional illness to the child by the spoonful.

Day after day, year after year. Until the invisible, unspoken brew goes smoothly down into the deep reaches of the child's soul and mind. Thus, the scapegoat accepts and swallows the fermented, toxic contents of the family fear and shame, thereby internalizing the heinous, contemptuous formula. It reeks of unlawful punishment--disguised as familial obligation.

The child has been appointed as the one to bear it all away... the decaying poison that will live on in the heart and counterfeit life of the innocent, yet obligated one. Unknown to the family–the constant toxins that infect the child is set to grip the carrier and become cemented in their inward parts.

The evil scheme uses the ignorance and pride of the families of origin to continue passing on the toxic shame to the next generation. The plan is to nullify and kill any Godly potential in this line of humans. Therefore, the scapegoat is isolated and cast out from the family formation–devoid of comfort, safety and support.

As the child progresses to adulthood, they must protect the contents of the internal containers of lies that they have ingested. Shame, guilt, fear, unresolved pain, unprosecuted crimes all must remain internally bound inside the bowels of the innocent scapegoat. There is no other recourse for the burden bearer. They must uphold the charade and successfully present as a functioning member of the family clan. The maintenance of appearances is primary to the toxic family. The cost to the scapegoat is their authentic life...spent forever protecting the toxic system in the name of 'family loyalty'.

To approach any member of the two-faced family system is to challenge the false front of the self-righteous blockade. They are united when it comes to defending against any 'disloyal accusations.' Even at the expense of the truth and what confronting the toxic family front might bring...namely emotional and mental health.

Undeniably then, asking for help or relief from the load that only continues to bloat the bearer, is absolutely and systemically forbidden. The truth, which is seen as a lie...must be kept always and only far away and outside the camp. The scapegoat must make their own way. She must manage the weight of the enablement of the colossal deception and the invalidation of her loved ones.

So then forsaken emotionally, unsupported, invalidated and unloved, the child must travel outside the perimeter of the family camp. Forced by unspoken rules and clamped down by expectations, the scapegoat, now an adult bears alone the incredible tonnage of lies. The continual, mandatory nature of her confusing and extremely oppressive assignment becomes fixed in her life. Never to be revoked or redeemed. The insidious, crushing arrangement renders ineffective and eliminates the authentic, Godly self of the family scapegoat.

Brainwashed and blinded into compliance by the onerous coat of shame, she bears the cursed burdens for the sake of the dishonorable family code.

Perhaps one day she will be set free from the horrendous assignment and come limping back into the fold of all she's ever known. It's a fleeting hope for the banished one. Without an intervention of catastrophic proportion—a breaking of the hold and power of the demonic spell...she, the scapegoat is set to wander forever. Outside of the real and marvelous plan of Godliness and peace that is intended for her life. Love and truth must take the place of the lost, burdened and lonely one.

Somewhere, an intercessor is praying, on behalf of the wandering, burdened scapegoat child, who is now a woman.

The intervention is coming.

Serpent and Systems

A Response to Scapegoat by Tom Josephson

The work of the enemy is seen in dysfunctional, unhealthy and frozen systemic strongholds. In the Garden of Eden, the paradigm was set.

The Enemy found the weakness in the first family system, and exploited it cunningly and completely. In the words of the comedian, Flip Wilson, "The devil made me do it."

This paradigm has been transmitted from generation to generation by a two-fold trap of parallel attacks, through Intergenerational Spiritual Curses and systemic psychological abuse. Either way, it leads to the emasculation of the self, in favor of the pseudo self, the fake self. The individual self is denied legitimacy in order to fulfill the role required for systemic stability. The force that propels this evil is shame – toxic shame.

Appropriate shame forms limits to bad behavior; Adam should have listened to God! Why he didn't is another story. Maybe he wanted to be the strong man who could do whatever he wanted showing off for his girl? But whatever his motivation, the shame of disobeying God's law didn't stop Adam. The preventative "shaming" of inappropriate behavior serves a purpose in society. When the guilty individual doesn't listen to shame in a preventative sense and goes and does what he and everyone knows is wrong, that shame is transferred into "shaming the personhood of the victim." In this way the system is intact, but "sick." The perpetrating adult gets to be "justified" while the victim gets to become the "cause" of his own victimization. The so-called "cause" is the fact that he "deserves" his victimization by virtue of the dysfunctional belief that the victim "IS" the "scapegoat or other "role: that now defines his causal identity.

Adam lied to cover up his shame of disobedience, which is appropriate guilt transformed into shame by the lie, guilt for doing what he knew in advance he shouldn't do. Had he not known that he was disobeying. the guilt could have stayed simply guilt for something done in error. But the foreknowledge that he was wrong required Adam to blame something else, because the absolute first rule is to protect the image the family wants to project. Phrases and philosophies such as:

"I'll do anything for my kids"

"It's for your own good"

"You know your father (or mother) loves you"

"If It was good enough for me, it's good enough for you"

"You think you're the only one to get (raped) in this family"

"What makes you think you're special (to want the freedom to be your true self)"

"Get over it already"

"If you tell anyone, you will be responsible for the demise of the entire family"

The system organizes around abuse, in whatever form it manifests. The children become expiators of the abuser's shame through such roles as:

Scapegoat

Martyr

Superstar

Hero

Sick one

Weak one

Really, any defined role serves some purpose in masking or deflecting or compensating for the abuser's shameful behavior and lack of shame. Consider this metaphor, a wind chime.

The windchime has various length strings that attach a variety of metal tubes to a platform. The tubes touch each other and make a musical sound when the wind blows them around. With no wind the windchime is level. What happens when you remove one of the tubes? The windchime becomes unstable, moving back and forth until a new equilibrium is gained. Usually, the entire windchime tilts in the direction of the missing chime. The resulting "stability" looks different. Now, there are chimes on top, some in the middle, and one at the very bottom. The "self-image" of the bottom chime is radically impacted. He will now feel less than. This is a natural property of systems of all kinds, restabilizing after a shock (change) that disrupts the status quo.

In this psychological dimension the self is sacrificed. Marcia's brilliant description of this process is detailed powerfully in her piece called "Scapegoat." Remember, the influence of systems in families is largely not consciously implemented.

My Outrage

When I was a child my parents both brought a load of their baggage to me. Each of them set their ugly, worn bags of personal effects down in my room—without a word.

I recognized both loads and I also knew that they meant for me to carry those bags—wherever I went. It was my job. Not just an unspoken mandate for me to interpret but it was also for me to assume the duty without question—no explanation. Just as with all the other rules—those spoken and those that were demonstrated—were assimilated into my soul…silently.

Each load was leaking poison. An extremely lethal and pervasive poison.

The sexual trauma that I had suffered at the hands of another male family member was a demonic gateway into my child's soul. Incest. It plowed a channel deep into my inward parts and psyche—therefore causing me to believe that I deserved to carry the malignant cargo—their toxic pain.

The noxious flood that it launched into the channel in my soul from each parent mixed there with my own shame. And fear.

My silent but resilient sense of responsibility as firstborn required me to bear that cargo of parental toxic pain and anger.

The silence that clouds and follows the sexual betrayal of a child cemented into my emotional center the colossal lie—that the shame was mine.

All of the noxious weight bearing down in me during my formative years wanted to become a permanent resident and character trait. It knew that...as a child—I would believe the lies. That I was shame and only always would be shameful. I was now the carrier and protector of something monstrous that threatened to condemn and sentence me to a lifetime of being the family scapegoat. I was innocent but the evil doubled down...destroying my self-worth, self-esteem and self-love. I was lost.

As I grew the weight of the lies and dysfunction in the bags and my personal agony only became heavier and more burdensome. And more difficult to keep concealed. My authentic self was being covered and slowly being eliminated. I was becoming conformed to the posture of a scapegoat and my stance was turning to stone. I had to shift the weight in order to function and appear as an adult in order to continue to comply with the deceitful pretense.

One venom filled bag was slung over each shoulder. This shift freed my hands so that I could put them to use finding what I naively thought life had for me. Every attempt to move forward and become productive was thwarted and sabotaged by the cumbersome travesty I continued to carry for the sake of family loyalty.

The personal pain of unprocessed sexual trauma, the silence of invalidation and their effects only increased the pressure of the load I was carrying to protect the enablers, people that were supposed to love me and protect me.

There was never any assistance or break from the burden bearing. There was constant terror buried alongside the truth of what had devastated me. Bringing the horror to the light of day would only be met and invalidated by vehement denial. It was useless.

As I attempted to fill my hands with the work of my own life–the contamination in the bags and my soul threw my life out of joint and took away my balance continually.

I was duty bound to the pressure and load–I truly believed the lies…still. The sordid and unlawful mission of my life remained unspoken and unresolved.

UNTIL–I heard the voice of the Son of God saying gently to me–'Set the bags down–give Me the burdens in your heart and soul and FOLLOW ME.' Of course, I said, 'Yes, Lord' I loved Him so…since His love had broken through to me on the basement floor in my parent's house…my large hard back Children's Bible in my lap…when I was very young.

'I'm coming I said but I can't set the bags down–I'm strong enough–I'll continue to carry them and protect my family secrets; I can't live without them…I can keep up!'

Following the Lover of my Soul–my heart and hands became full…full with the love and devotion for a man and two beautiful children.

It finally was too much. Too much to carry and still be able to follow and love Him and them well.

I came to the end of my strength. The particular toxins carried in each bag were leaking out all over me. I knew they would soon infect my marriage and my children.

One ragged bag held all kinds of pain, shame, and fear. An idol, symbolically representing loyalty to the multi-generational family system was particularly burdensome, akin to carrying a heavy, bulky piece of lead everywhere I went.

Keeping up appearances was the incense burned at the base of that horrendous masquerade of a healthy, fully functioning clan. The idol demanded undying loyalty and child sacrifice. One defector could blast the interlaced facsimile wide open. How would the family function if the truth were laid bare? The strength and power of it was fueled by self-righteousness, denial and abandonment.

The second bag of parental pain smelled musty and putrid as if something was dying inside. It was full of the usual components as well. Pain, shame and fear. And a sacrificial altar. The High Priest of the family sacrificial system was named. Worthless. He was in charge of sacrificing human, God-given potential on its grisly altar.

I was spending my God-given life blood trying to manage the weight of the historical toxicity and my own pain while keeping it all secret. It was never mine to carry! I so needed to be delivered to that truthful revelation!

The weight of the burden and the slow, constant drip of infected secrets mixed with the plagues that bear down on those suffering with childhood sexual trauma and incest finally threw me spiraling down into an exhausted dysfunctional heap.

I had been swimming in a murky swamp most of my life but now I was being pulled under. The demonic lies I believed were now becoming ankle weights that even the strongest swimmer could not outlast.

'Lord!' I cried! 'I want to cast off this titanic weight and load of catastrophic lies that I've been living with and coddling.'

'I want to live in the truth of who You created me to be and start living out the potential You gave me as a birth right.' 'Could it be that I must set the poisonous weight down and walk into your arms fully? 'I will leave all the unholiness at Your feet and finally find justice! For me!'

I was born to be a healer—not a pack mule of ungodly pain and demonic systems of idol worship.

'Father—fix in me the reality of Your grace. Fix it solidly in my mind and heart and emotions. Please reshape the strength You've given me and open my hands and arms to that grace. Let me take it in fully and own it.'

'I'm your Braveheart. I've always been your Braveheart. I want to live in that truth!'

She's a Healer

I was born with a golden essence deep within. My real and invariable nature was God-breathed into my soul. My destiny was imprinted upon and manifested in my uniqueness. It was a living entity, a developing force in my inward parts… enabled and ignited by the Holy hands that formed me in the womb. The absolute truth of who I was made to be.

So lies the divine potential that every human holds in store…in trust…waiting to be discovered and nurtured by those assigned to the care of His Masterpiece…this child.

I would become the brilliant and precious reflection of the loving and creative Master's hands and heart.

My true and noble portion resided deeply within me and sparkled brightly in my eyes. As I grew and learned to embrace the true essence of myself, I would learn that whatever I put my hands to during my Earthly days would be the fruit of the truth in my core.

There was a devious plan however… to disrupt, divert and destroy that golden essence. The God breathed destiny in me was seemingly lying unprotected, ignored and neglected by the very ones chosen to protect me.

Evil made its move.

Many years later I saw it as in a dream...at three or four years of age...I was standing alone on a sunny beach of a small, deserted island.

My first love, my Earthly father–brought me there and then sailed away...back to his island. To guard and care for and protect his first love...his mother.

Brave Heart–that small, beautiful child with the golden essence... needed much more than he was able to give. He was my all-in-all. My security and peace were wrapped up in Him. But I was forced to wait in line for his love, his attention, his support and validation. I watched him sail away–time and time again...not understanding that he was forever lost to me. In my child's mind I always held out hope for his return and his sweeping me up and into my fulfilled expectations.

He did return often to the shore of my island where I constantly stood waiting. He brought clothing and food but he never gathered me to himself...he never took me home with him. He broke my heart with his failure to fill my longing for acceptance, nurture and encouragement.

If he recognized my golden essence, it remained unknown to me. His attention was always focused on the distant shore of his other island.

So...I continued to stand alone on that sunny yet lonely beach–learning, adapting and becoming accustomed to my lonely state of survival.

Over the years it became my normal–standing alone, growing alone–not knowing that I could recognize and grow into my golden self.

The gap in my soul grew deeper and wider as time passed—until the difference between the recognition of and the development of my destiny became a bridgeless chasm. Survival became the primary driving force in my life leaving significance and importance in the distance.

I had been left to evolve and invent my own survival skills. It was all that he had to model to me.

The break in my self-esteem, had been pierced open by emotional neglect and it expanded into an acute vulnerability.

When the perversion came to me and soaked itself in my defenseless soul and inward parts—my gifts and my sparkle were immobilized by the quick drying cement of shame.

The attention I so greatly hungered for soured within me and it morphed into black, tar-like toxic mortification.

The perpetrator shed his shame onto me and into me.

The violation was swift and complete. Another victim had been created. More God-given destiny was now muted and stolen and decimated. So thought the evil.

The shining soul left alone on that shore of emotional neglect and desertion had never been truly alone. Until now. Overlooked by those given to protect and cherish me.

The abandonment had opened the door wide. I was ripe for abuse—for molestation—for incest—for the rape of my childhood.

Evil sought to do its utmost to destroy the hope and light in that child filled with gold.

I was contorted now with an adult awareness. I now believed I filled the role of cast-off completely. The opportunity to begin recognizing the gold within me was now aborted. Heartbroken and frozen in the false beliefs I now held about myself.

Somehow though–underneath the black tar coating of shame and the deadly misconceptions and untruths–the golden part of me remained untarnished and pure…that real part of me was shouting–screaming, pleading for recognition and release!

The divine Breath of God that had imparted the image of Himself into me…in my mother's womb…it had remained intact through everything! It was immutable! Just as He is!

My Heavenly Father's loving ideal had formed His hand-iwork in me and it could not and would not be rescinded or rejected by Him! He would not discount or discard the golden part of this child. It will never be counted as null or void! It was eternal and it belonged to Him.

The golden essence in me–conceived and written into the core of my personhood, my God-likeness was given and sealed within me. No matter what. The potential always remained–unsullied, uncorrupted by evil. It waited to be fulfilled…to become my destiny–who I really am and who I will become!

Braveheart, my true self, had been deserted and victim-ized…left alone…but the power of the life, death, shed blood and Resurrection of the Lord Jesus Christ kept me alive and moving. He is our ever living Intercessor and He was minister-ing on my behalf–in the stead of those who had left me alone. The Anointed One was moving upon the hearts of His Earthly intercessors also. For my sake. There were perhaps many that were beseeching and trusting Him for my freedom…without even knowing me personally.

Braveheart first became aware of Him and of His presence and love while standing alone on the beach of that deserted island during childhood. I recognized Him as He opened the eyes of my understanding that lay undeveloped in the golden part of myself. He graced me with the awareness of Himself and I loved Him in return. The power of His love and grace broke through my evil induced isolation and despair. It was then that I sensed it before I understood it. The golden part of me—created by Him…my destiny…who I really am…had remained…it was there all along…untarnished.

I only lacked the tools—the confidence—to grasp the truth as mine and own it. Absorb it fully. I believed myself to be most undeserving of any such reward because of the hidden and hindering tendrils of shame.

Still, I was driven, motivated and lead by a deep knowing and desire to discover the golden part of myself. The Son of God gave me, Braveheart, the unceasing, unrelenting desire to search for the parts of myself that remained living and crying out loudly for release and recognition. They were hidden and muted but always longing to be put to work for His Kingdom.

Then, after years of running yet seeking, longing for and then…reaching for what seemed to be just out of my grasp… the reconciliation was suddenly, stunningly there! The restoration between my conscious self and my golden destiny was at last before my very eyes.

Incredibly, massive amounts of unholy clutter began to dissolve, dissipate and make way and open wide for the Truth!

With the power of the grace that enabled me I found and opened the bottom drawer of my scarred psyche and I released my long-lost outrage along with my downhearted self-respect. This new plateau of freedom that I had reached, brought at last, my release from the long battle with the shame that had been unlawfully poured into my soul in order to make it become my own. I recognized the morbid container that had brought it to me...inflicted itself upon me. To kill me. One way or the other. The hold of the falsehood had robbed me of the life giving, pure, God-given truth about who I was, to whom I belonged and who I was going to be! The power of the immense deception was broken! I saw the truth and absorbed the truth and believed the truth!

I saw at last the value and preciousness of myself. I began to lay claim to it—all of it! The golden self, the unchanging part of myself that belonged forever to the Creator, had been there all along—unchanged by evil—flourishing and shining brightly!

I began the journey of coming home fully to my destiny... my identity in Christ. I am Brave Heart. I always have been but now I am living it. Jesus Christ is now the mirror in which I see the reflection of my true self.

His love is the sparkle in my life and eyes. My golden essence will never perish. It will always remain alive with Him.

My destiny—who I was born to be—is a mirror of that love. That healing, restorative love. Steadfast, never changing or ceasing love. The same power that enables and holds the Universe holds me.

My message now and forever is, please my friend, open your heart to His love. Ask Him to reveal your golden essence—the truth about who you are to become. You will never regret the journey because on the way you will come to know Him. Jesus Christ. And your journey will end in His arms always.

THE PAIN SPONGE

It originates in the deepest parts of the sexually traumatized child. A reflex initiated by the intense and excruciating fear and shame–shoved down mercilessly into the inner parts of her. The godless acts perpetrated on her have spawned a desperate need to cover and absorb the shame and terror thrust into her. It's a driving need that becomes a compulsive, unconscious habit. She's not born with it–it's not instinctual but the habitual use of it for the sake of survival causes it to become second nature...to cope...it's a means of survival.

How does her immature psyche continue to develop and perfect such a soul-deadening mechanism?

Why is it that her belief is now false...that SHE is shame... and because of that curse she must protect the adults she loves from knowing that her soul is being painfully shredded?

She accumulates and holds her own pain captive and does the same for everyone she knows and even for those she doesn't. No one must know. It locks her down...shame is accomplishing its deadly mission.

She must contain the pain...coddle it–at all cost to herself... this is her absolute. Her job–her mission. The pain and shame will kill them she mistakenly believes...but she can bear it...no matter how unrighteous and cruelly it festers.

Soon…the secret nature of the 'pain sponge' operates unconsciously and automatically. She swings into full pain absorption mode at a moment's notice… making space in her heart and soul for the pain of others. Why not? After all she has the capacity…or so she believes–to absorb and hold their pain as well as her own. It's becoming her life's purpose and secret work…keeping caverns in herself open to alleviate the proper processing of a suffering person…

She becomes the self-appointed keeper of the wells containing pain for others. To spare them she believes…it's the vehicle by which she wrongfully believes also that she will somewhere, somehow find her value, her self-worth.

It's a colossal, deadly lie. It's a cover up and it serves only to cripple her emotionally and it almost kills her physically. She only becomes more numb and all the while she is morphing into a flaming co-dependent…robbing herself and those whose pain she's carrying unlawfully. She sees no other recourse though…she is trapped in this silent existence…rationalizing that it is her mission. She feels she has no right to speak the truth and the truth has become as foreign to her as a lost and forgotten language.

The adult Pain Sponge has been in operation for so long that she barely recognizes the fact that she is strangling…crippled and lost in confusion. A thick fog of shame holds the putrid falseness in place. Withhold the truth–spare them the pain…it has become criminal now…withholding evidence and obstructing justice. The pain sponge has robbed the victim and herself of the opportunity to hold, process and resolve their own agony.

What she reckoned to be love—is far from it. How does she break free and give the pain back to its rightful owner?

Open my eyes Lord...the eyes of my heart and my understanding. Examine me and make me so aware of the harm I've done... to myself and others. Help me untwist what has me bound. Help me bring it all to You.... At the foot of the Cross. Help me to unload it and leave it all there with You. It's between You and my loved one. Help me depart from the distractions and the old, unproductive habits that only bind. I want to be free of the sickening mess. Help me make my own mess my priority and leave my loved one in Your hands.

You alone have already carried every pain and bucket load of shame—for all of us! You have resolved it all! At the Resurrection! You have reached beyond where any of us could reach and have resolved it! Be the Lord of my mistaken identity and keep me mindful of the retirement and demise of the pain sponge in my soul.

Lord—show me how to live without this non-functional, outlawed and counterfeit way of living and dealing with life. Show me who I truly am and how to truly love and assist someone in pain.

We need You, Lord!

Pain of Shame

There is pain in my soul....and in my mind. Sometimes it is a dull ache–sometimes a sharp stab. Many days it screams but mostly it's a persistent whisper. I built a room to store it in many years ago...thinking that keeping it hidden would make it manageable... even perhaps I could put it to death by denying it. But pain can ebb, be medicated, or tolerated, but it never dies. It can only be redeemed.

The love of my life became a man...so that He could become acquainted with my anguish, grief and sorrow. What I can't even name...He knows. What is too horrible for me to allow–He bore and carried in my stead. What's too wonderful for me to believe is that the severe punishment He endured for my health, peace and life was His destiny to fulfill.

Because of the bloody stripes on His back, I'm free...every whit whole...Lord...in You is the place to live and thrive...to be everything You've created me to be...Your masterpiece. The truth is that I belong to You and this certain assurance won't let me quit or give up on Your dream for me.

You are greater than the pain...Lord over the pain...You are the redeemer of the pain. Help me learn to help others to identify and sort through the pain. So, they can separate the pain from who they truly are...Not to merely cope but to overcome! Looking always to You—the Ultimate Overcomer…the Resurrected One…who gives His grace, mercy and favor freely and without fail.

ULTIMATE DECEPTION

You took full advantage of my innocence and trust. The diabolical abuse of your free will empowered your evil intentions.

You used that perverse power to perform the ultimate betrayal upon me.

You, my own flesh and blood—nineteen years old and someone I trusted with my seven-year-old heart.

You left the pernicious effects in my immature psyche—unloading your own heavy toxicity into my innocence and onto my child's body.

You caused ruinous, destructive and poisonous shame to consume me, blind me, mute and confuse my seven-year-old soul.

You were willing to harm and distort me to somehow soothe or relieve your own insidious corruption.

The enemy of my soul used you in a malicious attempt to destroy my relationship with Jesus and extinguish any indication that I belonged to Him.

The perverse tool of incest was intended to demolish any trace of Godliness and freedom in my life and to convolute the fact that He loved me unceasingly, unconditionally.

My true self was under attack–the goal was to invert and confuse me mentally, emotionally and spiritually. The potential and plan for a wondrous life of purpose and fruitfulness was His design for me…the birthright of every person–born with the image of Almighty God blueprinted in their soul.

My Godly destiny was waiting for me to grow into it.

Instead–I was subjected to living in the muck and mire of shame…concocted of false beliefs and twisted concepts of reality.

The ultimate deception consisted of the colossal lie that I swallowed. It manifested into a victim mindset…on course to see that the only fruit of my life would be self-loathing and frustration. I would live always outside of the beautiful plan for my life and the constant sting would be that I knew it.

Part two of the colossal lie is that the sexual trauma was my fault and I therefore negated and cancelled my pure relationship with the Good Shepherd.

I was deceived into believing that He had abandoned me. His lost lamb was caught in a wide and deep ditch full of brambles and thorns…holding me and tearing me apart.

I was destined now to exist and cope as a specter, a shadow of my true self in my shell of a life.

My only future was one of secret keeping…protecting and upholding the sick system that had infected me.

The Truth was however–never far from me! Magnificently… beautifully…powerfully…My Good Shepherd never let go of my unjustly soiled and damaged self! He would not let those monstrous inequities stand and hold me tightly forever!

The Eternal, fixed and invariable truth of who He is and the power of His sacrifice for you and I is the cure!

His shed Blood and Resurrection power and grace is the everlasting remedy that will and does blast apart the darkness and morbidity of that futile deception!

When He died, He took my misplaced shame, confusion and every damnable lie with Him to the pit of Hell where it belongs and left it all there.

He then ascended with the keys to Death and Hell in His nail-scarred hands…thereby completing the great exchange for us!

The power of the ultimate deception has been shattered and voided. Only the illusion remains! See it Beloved One!

His Blood has purchased freedom for everyone left alone in their pain!

Come with me friend! Shake off the lies, the misconceptions. Embrace Him! He is the Truth!

Take His hand along with me. He will never let go. Walk in everlasting peace and freedom. He is the Lord!

FAMILY LOYALTY

I deally a wonderful concept. Strength, support, validation and comfort. A warm and accepting place to lean into... where emotionally healthy, safe people would hold our hearts. A refuge from the cruel, vicious world. For a lifetime.

Realistically–it can become and remain a toxic trap. How does the family system become a deadly network of aiding and abetting liars, enabling perversion and covering up crime? How does the fallen human condition become the dominant force...overriding faith, hope, love and fidelity...and instead drive members to turn and devour one another? For the sake of honor and appearances.

How do the generations move so far from the center of Godly plans and intentions that have been held for them since before time began?

Is it the continued compliance with an open or even covert attack of evil that keeps the door open? Is it the enablement of a subtle malicious predator? Why does the family fail to acknowledge it and destroy the lasciviousness at the root? The denial and continued allowance of it has burst open an inroad into the family system through that portal of human weakness.

It all allows the growth and development of a seemingly impenetrable hedge of thorns...that threatens to surround and choke out the Godliness and potential from the family and each individual. Once the thorny barrier is full grown…it also somehow begins to become invisible…amazingly accepted and permitted by those aware of the evil.

Where is the brave one who will not fail to push through the soul killing apathy implanted in the formerly fertile family ground? The one who will strike the imprisoning, deadly hedge of thorny ungodliness with the double-edged sword of the Spirit of Truth…rising up out of the underground cave of shame and fear… She will destroy the bristly, secret filled family hedge at its root!

The Brave One loves the truth and the Truth Bearer more than the barbed, unholy but familiar family stockade that is guarding the godlessness masquerading as health and peace.

Then… suddenly as she steps forward with her eyes wide open…the sword of the Spirit in her hand and her belt buckled with the Truth–the Lion of Judah roars His strength and vitality to support her resolve. His intent is to restore the family line as the limping but awakened warrior steps forward–hacking the spiky brambles…

She is opening a way into and out of the toxic trap…empowered by faith and love and mercy of Jesus Christ the Righteous One! As she advances, she opens up the way for those inside…

She cries 'Come on with me!' 'Run to Him!' 'Let's leave the dregs of this existence behind and give our hearts once again to Him!' 'He holds the Universe in its place. Let's serve and honor Him–with our hearts, hands and lives–forever!'

He is above it all and deserving of our true devotion and honor. We want to truly live! True living and purpose and strength are available for us! We can banish evil from our lives because He has conquered it all. We can live with Him and for Him! Forever!

JERICHO

How does a heart and soul that belongs to Christ turn a deaf ear and close their eyes to the obvious change that indicates internal suffering in their precious young one?

Their own unresolved trauma, abandonment, and wrong beliefs have locked them down and become paramount over dealing with the horrid truth...more important than the intense needs of their innocent one...

It's the practiced, perpetual indifference that morphs into petrified apathy...

Leaving them unapproachable and compassionless behind the wall that surrounds the toxic parent.

How much has my own heart been hardened and damaged by being ignored, invalidated, unsupported and forced to conceal the horrible truth of crimes committed against my body and personhood?

Compelled by shame to view and live out a life of pretense as normal–acceptable and especially 'required.'

Could my child's soft, pure heart be brought back and restored to me?

Where is affection? How does love feel? Is it more than just mental assent?

Will the hard corners in my soul always remain vacant?

In silence...shame stunted me...emotionally. Forced to comply...muted...perfecting the motions to fulfill the expectations.

Then–miraculously–the love and grace of my Redeemer has come...His glory blazing...shining His light and love–scattering and destroying the fog and layers of shame...I have finally reached the very end of myself and my self-deception of strength. I fall to my knees...

He has answered the cry of my entire being–turning my desperation to hope and my misery into harmony...in step and in agreement with my Good Shepherd and my Helper who leads me into the Truth...and they say...

'Step out of and away from the cloak of shame–you're wearing it unlawfully My precious child.' 'You have believed but struggled with the colossal lies!' 'Believe Me now and forever!'

'I will make your aching heart secure again!'

'I will make firm your foundation that evil intended to weaken and destroy '

'I will show you how to live an authentic life...with Me at the Helm...guiding you always.'

'The terror that has tortured you will be turned into a calm and peaceful life...filled with everlasting fruitfulness...in My hands.'

'Confidence and self-respect will lead the way for you...into the life of service you have always envisioned and longed for.

'I have paid the price so that you may honor our Father by living a quality Earthly life openly–without secrets and pretense.

He said also—'The sexual trauma has attempted to lock you inside a fortress as seemingly impenetrable as Jericho once was. Abominations were committed there and it did not stand. So, Rejoice!'

'Jericho sought to keep you bound to do its bidding...living out the falsehoods of lies and shame. But I have delivered you forever with My mighty roar of freedom and My Shepherds strong staff of righteousness.'

'Jericho's deceptive walls are broken down and decimated. See your freedom! 'Take firm hold of it!'

'Walk always with Me now and believe only the Truth about yourself and about Me!'

'I am the Lord!'

GOD IN THE FIRE

A Response to "Jericho" by Tom Josephson

Where else could it come from
if not the belly of the stars
bursting
across the numb
word?

The fire in the bush
across centuries?

The punctuation in the raised hands
of the prophets
of the distressed?

The wonder in the eyes
of the child
who first see twigs
incinerate mighty trees
in the primal firepit?

The pain become rage
and melt into prayer
in a chorus of angels?

The voice in the mirror,
the fire of awareness,
has brought forth
Glory from among us!

Surely, God is in the fire!

CHINA

The inescapable reality of the immense mass of humanity in Hong Kong and on the mainland of China was daunting in every aspect.

How is it possible to make a solid, lasting inroad of difference in this sea of poverty and suffering? It seems unfathomable. Yet, noble. It appeals greatly to my Western sense of adventure.

Therein lies the duality of my mission, or could it be the confusion of culture shock? As I view the landscape and the virtual sea of humanity personally, I am overwhelmed. But my intent is mission driven and fixed, I reasoned.

Then again, I wonder, *what am I doing here, really?* I thought my motives were clear and true. Am I correct in my assumption that my purpose here is predicated upon the need? We are Americans. Of course, we know how to fix things and we have the means to do so. That makes us right…wait, what?

I arrived at the orphanage that day, with my Western, American idealist viewpoint intact. Then, I entered the spartan, austere, and cold facility. It has the appearance of a fortress. The structure was now serving as a home for cast off and abandoned children, orphans, and the elderly.

Our team members, motivated by mercy, came into that empty back room on that chilly April morning and I saw him.

A newborn, alone, whimpering, disfigured and left to die. He was nearly naked and lying in front of an open window. I was stunned. How can this be? This innocent one was left alone to die?!

Every instinct in me screamed! His life is precious and valuable simply because he exists. Help him! There were no means or desire though to prolong his suffering or to repair the rupture in his spine. So said those in charge of the orphanage. He had been abandoned. Probably by his parents. His birth defect was too large and profound to fix. The greatest show of mercy was to let him go peacefully.

The only apparent recourse available to soothe him and soothe myself was to comfort him somewhat with a warm water bottle wrapped in a bit of blanket and placed next to him. There was no reversing the inevitable. His agony and pain lasted only a short time longer. He moved on from this cruel place into the arms of the Good Shepherd.

The stark disregard for that disfigured baby was difficult to come to terms with. My American, Western, Judeo-Christian filter could not reconcile what I believed to be true with what I was witnessing. Life is precious. Every life. How does it happen? What I'm witnessing is a crime in my country.

His death would be balanced by the many more children born tomorrow in this land of billions of souls they said. This abandoned child's life and death was viewed simply in a matter-of-fact manner here, halfway around the world from my home.

Twenty-five years have passed since that April morning. The abandoned, crippled child has been in the arms of the Good Shepherd all this time.

I've been in the midst of recovery from childhood sexual trauma for many years since. The abandonment that dysfunctional family systems perpetuate to cover the shame of sexual trauma has been almost more difficult to process and overcome than the trauma itself.

As I heal, layer by layer, I have gained perspective on the short life of that precious, crippled newborn in that orphanage in China.

I can say in all actuality, that my recovery and restoration began there with the short life of that living example of cruel abandonment.

I went to China fully intending to help soothe the pain of some forlorn ones living there. I believe now that it was the Lord's dual intention to use me to give comfort and to give me an unmistakable human illustration of what was lying in the bottom drawer in my soul, covered over. The accumulation of my pain, coupled with and multiplied by my family's pain, shame and fear. And my own abandonment.

Reflecting now I see that his short life and death spoke out loud, in volumes, about the inability in effect, of our human effort to resolve our own distress and chronic dysfunction and abandonment. I was running, trying to soothe and absolve my own pain of abandonment, buried deep by attempting to soothe and cure the pain of others.

It has taken a long time, and much has been uncovered since discovering the pitifulness of the human condition in real time. I bear the imprint of that child in my soul.

But the Lord didn't leave me there in that place of unresolved, fatal neglect and death. The power of the duality of the purpose of my missionary journey resonates in my heart. By His grace I have continued to move forward into the plan of freedom for my life.

Thank you, Father. Because you love me You wouldn't allow me to live that hollow life of abandonment, neglect and victimhood. By Your grace I'm empowered to keep coming, moving toward You and Your eternal destiny that has always been planned and available to me.

Deliver me once again from falseness and give me the courage to become me. Fully and truly me.

I'm on my way. Fully relying on your grace. I'm grateful for the short but precious life of that crippled child. The life changing effect of his brief time on Earth, helped to initiate the needed change in me.

Please keep transforming my point of view into Your point of view. Thank You for bringing me back across the water. To my life. My family. My life in You. I know with an assurance that I will soon see Your face first and then his. We will always be together. In your everlasting embrace.

THE BABY BY THE WINDOW

A response to China by Tom Josephson

A great friend went to China on a mission trip
twenty-five years ago,
and recently recalled:

"It was in one of the orphanages
where I saw something
I can't get out of my mind.
It was overcrowded and understaffed;
it was a terrible sight.
A tiny infant with a large deformity
dominating his tiny back,
lay shivering, alone, near a window,
crying, and waving his tiny arms in the air,
but no one was there;
he was all alone.
everyone left him there,
alone and cold and abandoned.

The abandonment inside me erupted.
I know that terror,
I know that shame.

I had no authorization,
but I had to comfort that poor baby
in the little time we had to share,
and when we left,
I left that tiny precious one alone,
to die, mercifully, and rest in God's arms.

I still see his tiny body in my mind.
There is so much pain, so much sorrow,
his little life reminds me.
It's time I honor that baby near the window,
and honor Jesus, Who healed my soul,
after twenty-five years of bearing the pain of shame
that lay heavy on me,
like the huge hump on that tiny baby's back,
and bring God's comfort in deed and word
to others alone in the cold.

That shall be my ministry.
The Lord is oh so worthy!"

My Heritage

Their blood is my blood. Their DNA is alive in me.

The call to greatness echoes in my heart and soul—tempered with humility and executed with purposeful intent. Their service and loyalty were rewarded with lands and titles. They battled and served and conquered with great men. They died in the Crusades following their ideals. Their line prospered and continued moving forward.

They crossed the Atlantic and helped create a new colony and a new nation. They pioneered westward and suffered the loss of their patriarch. They met and married. They homesteaded. They broke hard, virgin ground. They carved out a new life and survived hardships on the prairie. They built and maintained a small town in the midst of their farmstead.

They bore and raised many children…and suffered the loss of some of them—at birth and in infancy. They enjoyed grandchildren. They endured to an elderly age.

Their blood and DNA and the drive of mission are all my heritage. They were all given a special assignment—some noble and some ignoble…all conceived and directed by the Hand of Providence.

Out of countless souls they were chosen for a unique purpose. They were all bestowed with a heart to undertake each task–great or small...noteworthy or seemingly insignificant. Through the years...the centuries, the oceans crossed, the miles traveled by ox and wagon...Have all culminated and reached their zenith...here...in my heart...in my dreams and my own sense of mission and destiny.

I see the Captain of our souls as I look back at the arc of time and I realize that as much as it is our story–it is more His... His truth...His reality...His voice...His hands...moving and directing and guiding this family...both ancient and current... into His plan...His design...for this one line of humanity.

To grow and to keep going–into His ultimate, beautiful purpose–for His sake...His glory. All of our dreams...desires and passions spring from His heart. His dreams for us to really live and to understand that His desires for us are deep and wide.

The fulfillment of the human experience–to live authentic lives–from our hearts that belong to Him. That was and still is His mission...to lead us and guide us into the fullness of the goodness that Christ died to give us.

That is the legacy we can leave for those we know will follow us–warriors and patriots and pioneers still...forever finding our way...following the paths and roads laid out before us...with His mission in our hearts and minds. To live and grow and to keep on going...with Him by our side and with Eternity in view.

THE RESOLUTION THE RESTITUTION

B efore I was born there was a design…a blueprint in the mind and heart of Almighty God. For my life. Time spent on Earth and in the timelessness of Eternity. As a child I was introduced to Him and was aware of His presence from then on.

Before sexual trauma incinerated my childhood, He was very real to me. Before I became the scapegoat in my familial system, I knew Him.

At the age of twelve I made a public but very personal commitment of my life to Him. I gave Him my heart. Gratefully, thankfully. I knew beyond a doubt that He loved and wanted me to walk with Him. I belonged to Him.

By the age of eighteen I was letting Him slip away…I thought.

Unresolved sexual trauma and generational transgressions ruled my life internally but no one knew it from my outward expression.

Fear and anger and shame were driving me from a secret hideaway located deeply in my soul.

Through those years of pain and pretense I always recognized His voice. I was keenly aware of the gentle touch of His

Shepherd's staff...nudging me back to my life in Him. My real life. His design for me.

He never ceased to call my name and His arms were always open wide.

I was near death and He brought me out of its's dark grip. He sealed the restoration of my health with an appearance of His manifest presence. Like a banner over me in my hospital bed–His glory shone like a sparkling cloud and gave my mother the assurance that I would indeed live and not for a short spell.

Strength was restored to me physically but my heart was still far from Him...wrapped in fear.

The guilt and shame and everything that I misunderstood about myself stood as a seemingly impenetrable barrier between He and I. Or so I reasoned.

My life belonged to Him in love but my heart mistakenly believed that I could never become who He meant for me to be.

My destiny was to become what had been perpetrated upon me...so said shame.

So, I ran...the guilt drove me down many roads and to many lonely places in my young adulthood.

Until one winter night...His love and longing for me broke through the muck and mire of my defenses. The power of His presence...love upon love upon love...empowered me to make a turn...fully toward Him, never looking back. Forward toward victory and freedom...my true destiny...His design. I would become Brave Heart. A servant to His throne.

The journey moving forward has been constant yet not without obstacles.

Growing into the mantle of His love and truth has taken time, persistence and the support of a Gideon's army of loved ones…who have loved me truly.

The redemptive love of the Good Shepherd, the Lamb of God has shown me, yes, proved to me that His purpose has always been to reveal His Masterpiece in the block of marble… it's me. And it's you also my friend.

My mission now, as it always has been…is to extend His hand—my hand—to another hurting, misguided and cast aside lamb—wandering outside of His plan. Never unloved, never forgotten by Him.

Help me Lord with Your grace…show them who they really are and the magnificent blueprint You have waiting for them to live in, walk in. Now and in Eternity.

The Lamb of God, His finished work, His mercy, love and peace will enable us to keep moving forward toward more and more love and acceptance.

In Him there is no striving—only relaxing into the hands of The Helper. His astounding grace never ends or falls short. Our lives and hearts may belong to Him fully and completely without fear. Not from compulsion but out of gratitude. To live out of our love debt to Him.

Run to Him my friend. Stay with Him. Always.

CHOICES

T o be born female...not by chance but by design.
Blueprints of destiny and purpose are innate in her...
they originate with the Master Builder and architect of her
DNA.

Those plans manifest into hopes and dreams as she develops
into her personality and her body and mind mature.

There is a unique giftedness in the demeanor and manner of
her... precious child.

Who will endeavor to water and encourage the impartation
of greatness given to this beautiful girl?

Of course, they must notice the sparkle in her eyes. Her
countenance and her manner speak volumes as she reflects the
beauty of her Creator.

Her specialness radiates the work of the master craftsman
that formed her in the womb.

There is no pretense in this one...only a strong, clear reflection of His skill in the showing out of this masterpiece.

Who will notice and take care of and nurture and encourage
this endowment wrapped in human form?

Will they seek wisdom regarding how to develop the invest-
ment of greatness in this vulnerable young one?

Those chosen to care for her will establish and impose expectations and limits as she grows.

Tragically though...the protectors are distracted by life in general and discouraged by their own unfulfilled or underdeveloped giftedness.

Then...tragically–Evil notices her.

It's a devious and cunning living entity...looking for someone to devour.

The intention and scheme are to crush her, mute her and twist her giftedness into broken shreds until all hope is completely destroyed.

Incest.

A death sentence for the soul of one so abused, tormented and violated.

Where were those in charge of her care and protection? Where are they now...after the devastation and annihilation of her true personhood?

No one notices her excruciating despair as the wrongfully assimilated shame succeeds in covering over and completely masking her unique sparkle.

No one notices or pays heed to her pain or her withdrawal into isolation or disassociation.

Except that...her destiny was that she was born to belong to Christ...to love and follow Him. Somewhere, someone was being inspired by the Helper...the presence of God in the Earth...to pray and intercede for her...for young Brave Heart.

Her heart and soul were decimated and devastated. Her voice was muted and finally silenced.

But...it would not stand.

This one born with a golden, unchangeable essence would not truly be left alone.

Her missionary heart was still beating true allegiance to her Good Shepherd...she was His and He would never leave her or forsake her.

SHE STRUGGLES THROUGH THE HAZE

Where has my girl gone?

Though greatly troubled...love has always been your signature...

Love is your mode...

Love is your belief and love is the hope I cling to now...

As I watch your struggle from afar...

Love is the only message I can get to you now...

In prayer and supplication, I find my hope.

For in the One in whom I trust, there is a greater force and desire than my own–to cradle you in His arms, to reassure you...and to bring peace to your heart and mind and soul.

My trust and confidence are in Him...His arm is not too short...to lead you to freedom and resolution and deliverance from evil...along with any embedded effects from malice... whether you can recall it or not...

If my belief falls short of His ability or willingness to deliver His lamb...then His work is not finished and the power of His shed Blood falls short as well...it lies there on the Mercy Seat in the throne room of Almighty God...ineffectively staining the gold forever...

But...the work IS FINISHED! His blood does continue to save to the uttermost!

He says that No One shall take mine out of My Hand!

His words are true and everlasting...on that I can depend and place my trust...for you, my child, my love...even when all I see and hear points to the contrary of that righteous truth!

I will always walk by faith and not by sight...by the power of His grace.

He is the Lord!

SIMPLY BELIEVE

I t finally stops here...
The relentless search for self-esteem and worth.

A lifetime spent attempting to manufacture and maintain a functioning sense of self...

Constantly scrambling...chasing an elusive condition that was already there in my soul...

Covered and smothered by shame...waiting to be revealed and thrive.

Suddenly...I saw it standing there...arms open wide and singing to me–sweet melodies of Reconciliation and belonging.

'I was here all along'...self-love sang to me. 'I'm the gift from God that you've never opened'...

'We belong together forever.'

Then...I sensed Him there...close to me.

As He always was...'Simply believe' He said. 'This is the work of God...to simply believe in Me–the One whom the Father has sent.'

'Take the self-esteem, self-worth, and self-love that I came to give you...that I gave up my life for...they are the garments of your new personhood...dispose of the old, disgusting rags that you wore before you were recreated and came to live in and with Me.

'Walk in the newness of life that I purchased for you with my blood and sacrifice.'

'The garments of self-esteem, worth and love fit you well.'

He finished by saying 'Now remember who you are and who you belong to.' 'Give me the missionary heart that I gave you… commit it to Me.'

'Now you are dressed and ready to go…you have all that you need…'Now…Follow Me Brave Heart.'

John 6:29, NIV — 'The work of God is this–to believe in the One He sent.'

MINISTRY OF SHOWING UP

... **M**ost of all I'm allowing–inviting and welcoming in a change–to fix itself as my point of view. A component of growth that until now has been only a hope–an aspiration. The difference is now what I know to be true...in the very heart of me.

At last–I found the door to the deepest, darkest room in my soul. The place where my sense of self and esteem had been hidden away–chained up in shame and false beliefs.

I now believe what is true and meant for everyone–belongs to me.

The mantle of self-love and self-respect–paid for and delivered to me by the Blood and finished sacrifice of the Lamb of God. It has always been fitted and ready for me to wear since before I was born.

I opened that last cellar door and allowed that same redemptive blood to scour it and create a fresh room in my heart.

This mantle of righteousness is affecting and improving my inward vision and perceptions.

I've discovered and decided that it's way past time for me to safely remove you from the pedestal that I placed you on years ago.

My love and admiration for you is now able to set you safely on the ground–where we all live. No one could survive up there–at that altitude. The air is too thin and you've been an open target all alone.

I falsely believed that I could strive all my life and never come close to your God-given power...

Now I'm assured that your desire is to walk shoulder to shoulder and hand in hand...where it's safe.

You will be you and I am becoming me...as we walk forward arm in arm...with Eternity in view.

Iron Sharpens Iron

Proverbs 27:17, NIV,…as iron sharpens iron so one person sharpens another.…

Accountability. It can be a daunting requirement for a phlegmatic/sanguine temperament such as myself. It sounds like work. It is actually one of the most difficult things I've done, to make myself accountable. I don't mean in terms of personal integrity; I'm speaking in terms of soul work.

As a Believer, Lover, and Follower of Jesus Christ for over forty years now, I only want to draw closer and be all that I can be. As the saying goes. Not out of compulsion or guilt but because I know Him and I greatly desire my life to reflect His. Sincerely.

Am I human? Of course. Am I greatly flawed? Absolutely. But I love Him more. More than my own way. Do I have free will? Yes, it's the greatest gift He has given us. Have I abused my free will and hurt others and myself? Definitely. More than I would like to admit.

What then is the point of this essay?

Honestly, I have been on a journey most of my adult life, searching for myself. When I was young that was a catchphrase. During the 1960s many things in our society were changing.

People were falling out of their lives and going off somewhere to 'find themselves'.

So, what's different about my journey to find myself?

Friends–I was a victim of incest when I was a young child. My family of origin functioned as an emotionally stunted, locked down unit. Needless to say, I suffered the effects in silence. The greatest stranglehold was the toxic shame that is transmitted to the victim from the perpetrator.

My journey has been about how I coped and functioned as a half alive, mostly covered over child and I continued to live that way until well into adulthood. In fact, I was in mid-life

before I told my secret to the second person ever. When I had finally confessed to the abomination when I was in early adulthood, I was rebuffed and told to continue to keep it quiet.

After many years, the weight of the secrets became too much to bear. I had been a follower of Christ many years before I told the truth to anyone again.

I know and truly believe that it was NOT His desire for me to bear the burdens that the secrets created any longer.

He answered the cry of my heart and brought me to a safe helper. I was beginning to scrape the top layer of my pain off but I wasn't yet ready to reveal my secrets to the world. The shame that covers the victim twists and distorts the truth about themselves. One of my biggest problems was my false belief that I must hide the truth at all costs to protect those I loved from my shame. It was never my shame. I was the victim. I did nothing wrong.

Over the course of the next few years of my journey, I did go public with the truth and I did reach another plateau of health but…something was still missing…something still gnawed at me. 'What is it?' I asked myself and I asked the Lord.

Again, He met me right where I was.

I had always truly believed that I had a destiny, but with the lingering shame still blocking my vision and confusing my mind, I couldn't see the forest for the trees, as the saying goes. There was another level of mental and emotional health waiting for me, to attain it, grasp it, and claim it for myself. But I was at a colossal loss about how to get to that healing place that I only sensed was available to me. How do I get there, live there, stay there? Thrive there?

Then…I met a friend, the older brother that I had never had. He is an encourager, an exhorter, a life coach by profession but mostly by pure giftedness. He himself had suffered childhood trauma and abuse. He had reached an overcoming plateau in his life though, by grace, and he was now extending his hand to others. Reaching out to help bring them to that place of mental, emotional health and peace.

He quickly diagnosed the sickness still in my soul, the lack of self-worth, honesty, transparency that I was still holding onto. I didn't know how to let those stinking rags of wrong thinking, wrong responses and wrong actions go. What do I replace it all with? Those things had kept me alive and helped me survive the isolation and pain of my childhood and young adulthood. They were the dregs though that needed to go. But they were stuck…cemented into my soul by the toxic shame that had penetrated my psyche and belief system. Underlying the shame though was the real culprit. The stark terror that was force fed to me by the perpetrator and the family system I lived in.

The gift of accountability I spoke of consisted of the brutally honest confrontation that I held with the shame and the fear. Over a matter of weeks. Don't think it was easy but it was time. Way past time. The confrontation was facilitated by my brother and friend, who is also my brother in Christ. He and my husband and I witnessed miracle after miracle of honesty, release of pain and the letting go and elimination of toxic shame from my life. I found my long-lost outrage and my equally lost self-respect. I finally turned every corner I needed to turn and uncovered every filthy rag of misbelief about myself.

My greatest tool was my pen and a spiral notebook. I began not just journaling about what was happening but explaining it so that others could understand it. The result is that my brother and I have, along with my husband formed a company and we are publishing a collaborative collection of our writing. We have written about our personal battles and triumphs and our heart's desire is to assist others in their healing journey. We both know what it takes and we both know that you my friend can do it too.

The love and grace of our Lord Jesus Christ and the Helper, the Holy Spirit are the keys to health and life. Not only in the world to come but here. Now.

Join us friends in a life of living in the overcoming grace of our Lord. You are worth it. He is more than worth it.

WHAT MARCIA DID

by Tom Josephson

T his is not going to be in chronological order. As Marcia's life coach, it is my view that the relentless, courageous search-and-destroy mission Marcia undertook, that birthed her true self, her authentic self, out of the incubation of her past, her trauma, the change-back quicksand of family secrets and rules to protect those secrets from the light of day, from the light of awareness of Marcia herself, from her situation, and all that entails, and ultimately, from the Enemy, whose fury knows no bounds in the face of one rising up to authenticity, a life in the truth, in relationship with Jesus Christ, honoring and sanctifying the Holy, and ultimately, claiming Victory over victimhood, that Marcia has established herself as an overcomer of the first rank.

Marcia saw herself stuck in a swamp, so we went to that swamp. We examined the swamp, and Marcia said, "Can you help me out?" That very question was the beginning. The truth is, as a coach, I can and did, tell her from outside what things looked like, and what extrication could look like, but it was Marcia who took every step. The main tools I offered were encouragement, and a will to the truth, wherever that would lead.

There were so many conversations, exhortations, assertions, and every other kind of feedback, but the one constant was Marcia's will to find her authenticity, including her real pain, her real outrage, her real judgement of the behavior of perpetrators and enablers, and gradually, Marcia began to own those feelings and thoughts and discernment, and by naming and owning those feelings and judgments, Marcia began the process of letting them go.

I was surprised that she kept moving forward, because I know how tough it is. Marcia told me about knowing Jesus as a child. And how that love sustained her. She told me about her missionary heart, and about an impactful trip to China. She also told me she was inspired by the piece I had written about my mother, Sophie.

Marcia wrote "Scapegoat," a brilliant piece, explaining dysfunctional family systems, rules, and the devastating impact on the victim/scapegoat. Marcia finally named it, told the truth, that she was violated, abused, incested by a cousin, under the roof of her beloved aunt. And her outrage came forth.

She told the truth! Somewhere (John 8:32), in the Holy Book, the Lord Himself, says "The truth shall set you free."

There were periods of doubt, shame, projected anger, but always Marcia, sought freedom, the freedom to be her true self, ultimately the girl who loved and still loves, the Lord.

And she wrote Jericho, an amazing description of dismantling strongholds built by the Enemy, inside your own psyche, ostensibly to protect, but which trapped her inside the fortress of Shame. And then she took it down, because, as Jericho couldn't stand, neither could her own Jericho of Shame stand in the light of the truth. And it crumbled.

By this time, we had become a collaborative team, co-authoring this work. Marcia's writing helped her move toward Him, toward her true self, able to receive the Fulness of His blessings. A final hurdle presented itself. And it was BIG.

I wasn't sure how to approach it. But I told Marcia what I saw and asked if she would address it.

Marcia's love of the Lord has been consistent. She wanted and, in my opinion, has succeeded, in manifesting that love, pointing to it as her Salvation.

The issue was, given her beautiful depiction of the Lord's Love, and what it can do, and how she had laid her burdens on the cross, the reality was Marcia was still suffering from the pain, the anger, the thoughts, the pull of change-back behavior, all of it, despite her insight and awareness and love of Jesus. My concern was about giving false hope. That others might say, "Well, I've taken this to the altar, I've left it at the cross, but I still feel like I'm in the swamp, yet the indication I'm getting is taking it to the cross is sufficient...now I'm kind of feeling bad about that too!"

Then Marcia wrote "Iron Sharpens Iron," where she addresses this very issue. She tells our readers substantially what I've summarized above. She goes into the heart of the matter for her, which I believe is the essence.

She told the truth, the whole truth, and nothing but the truth. She had not fully released her shame and wasn't ready to until she could see it. Which is where I came in as her coach. Because like any other coach, the coach can see from outside what you inside can't see when you're in it. Even Tiger Woods has a swing coach. And when she told that truth too, she was finished.

It is like a rebirth. We have discussed these matters. Marcia has finished the work of this book. She has also shed all the entanglements that held her in the swamp.

There is a lot more to say about these matters, and Marcia has already started. I guess we are moving forward. Marcia's missionary heart has staked a new claim! We will keep you posted.

LIFE VERSE JOHN 6:27-29

W hen I was young—newly found by You and intoxicated with zeal and fervor and gratitude...

I promised my life to you—along with my heart.

I meant those words but I had no idea of course what lay ahead along the path I so wanted to walk on with You. I loved You so.

The dedication has never waned although it may have ebbed and flowed in the face of the realities that this life holds as the years pass.

Then, while on my way I saw John chapter six. So much happened in a short telling of events. Most tend to focus on the spectacular miracle of the feeding of the five thousand. Many sermons have been delivered regarding the Lord's ability to multiply and bless the average Christ follower's simple loaves and fishes.

I've not heard anyone speak about the words that Jesus spoke to the folks who had followed Him across the lake to Capernaum.

They questioned him about the time He had arrived on the far shore. Jesus didn't respond with the fact that His trip had been expedited because He walked on the water. Instead, He questioned them…about their motive for finding Him. More food. They were hungry again.

Then He says in verse 27–'Don't work for food that spoils. Work for food that gives eternal life. The Son of Man will give you this food because God the Father has given Him the right to do so.'

Then they asked Him–'What does God want us to do?' He answered–'God wants you to have faith in the One He sent.

The New Living Translation says it this way–Verse twenty-seven, 'But don't be so concerned about perishable things like food. Spend your energy seeking the Eternal Life that the Son of Man can give you. For God the Father has given Me the seal of His approval.

Verse twenty-eight, 'we want to perform God's works too. What should we do?'

Verse twenty-nine, Jesus told them, 'This is the only work God wants from you: Believe in the one He has sent.'

My heart said then–this is a life verse for you.

I questioned Him also, 'Lord, how can this be? Surely 'believing' can't be my career, my life's work?'

I was struggling mightily internally that time, as I had been most of my life. Distressed and uncertain, I was living a sub-par life of pretense. The effects of trauma and the secondary trauma of forced silence and incredibly cruel invalidation was punishing and it was strangling me.

After many years of following Him, loving and trusting Him I still felt totally disqualified from having a healthy, prosperous life.

I heard Him say to my heart then…'Consider the lilies of the field, they neither toil or spin. If my Father cares so much for them, how much more does He care for you?'

Could it be that the Father really loved me? I knew without a doubt that Jesus did love me because of all that He did for me but isn't the Father angry with me?

I couldn't break through the barrier of guilt. I couldn't abandon the defeat of self-loathing.

All I knew to do was to keep coming. Keep moving forward. I was chasing something I couldn't even name. But I knew something was waiting for me…waiting for me to step into, put on and in which to live.

Then I would remember…'Believe.' Just believe. Believing brought me to a place eventually where I began my fight for freedom. True freedom. True peace of mind. Security and self-assurance in my identity and walk with Christ. Authenticity. Transparency.

I spent twenty years believing, trusting and fighting. Fighting with the armor of the Lord, not in my own strength. He kept nudging me forward with His Shepherd's staff. I would have quit the fight without the drive to be healed.

Then, suddenly, I discovered and recognized my archenemy for what it was and how it had worked all my life to deconstruct my destiny and destroy my life.

Fear and shame were tireless, convincing me that I was worthless, and I always would be.

I finally told the truth about being sexually molested and named the perpetrators. I found my long-lost horror and my pent-up, deep anger. My child's mind had been stuck and was missing the clarity and resolve to resist and defy them. I took my life back. I am now living free and clear. Free from shame that was never mine to hold or preserve. Free from fear. Free to live the life I was born to live. To live fully as the person I was created to be.

I live in confidence and peace. And I simply believe.

MY HORIZON

I finally found the courage to stand my ground…
Now…where is the ground?
Is the view I see now my last horizon?
I still carry my hopeful dreams…
I still long to go beyond my past and present perceptions…
And witness the unfolding of Your grace in the lives of others…

So–I stretch my heart's eye above and beyond my current world of circumstances and I see an ocean of faces with outstretched hands.

Each one is vitally important and a treasure of my Father's design…

The staggering number of hopes and dreams each life represents drops me to my knees and I

Declare 'Lord be glorified!'…there just beyond my horizon…

Whatever part you have determined for me to play–help my heart to know and see as I move

Forward once again…trusting in Your holy plan.

You hold every soul in its place… to accomplish Your master design of goodness, faith and love.

Oh Lord–enable my eyes of faith to see my part–to touch hearts and lives and souls with Your peace and promise.

WHAT ELSE IS HAPPENING?

by Tom Josephson

We did a great work, Marcia and I,
with Roger's full support every step of the way.
I must mention my wife, Loretta,
who is every bit the same level of support in her way.

What happened during this process,
was Marcia coming all the way through,
all the way through to the truth of who she is.
A stunning achievement!

As Marcia found new levels to explore
it opened up new possibilities for me to coach her as well.
Iron sharpens iron is a two-way process.
I have grown, both emotionally and spiritually.
My walk in faith has become more and more natural.
Roger and Marcia are the real deal in that regard.

The steps, which I described in "The Right Path"
Explain the process in outline form;
But I believe it is also a blueprint
for a community of families in Christ.
I can see people coming here at some point,

breaking bread in Ryan's Cathedral,
this safe spirit-filled space.

I can see people finding their truth
in real fellowship.
Marcia, Roger, Loretta and I are as different
as people can be in demographical terms.
Roger is from the farm in small town Iowa.
Marcia is herself a small-town girl who
wanted to make music. Her writing is lyrical.
Roger is practical. I am born a Jew, the son of Holocaust survivors,
first generation born of immigrants, I was raised in the Bronx,
right next to the Marble Hill Housing Project.
I grew up in an urban world.
Loretta is a black woman from South Georgia,
raised through difficult times.
I have begun to know some of Marcia and Roger's friends.
They have met some of my friends when we are on the phone.

My neighbors in Brunswick, Georgia are excited about
our podcast.
This joining of two families is taking root, I believe, in the rich
supernatural soil called the Holy Spirit.

We all wish the very best for each and every one of you.

In His name!

THE SPIRAL ARM OF MEANING

by Tom Josephson

We live about 28,000 light years from the galactic center,
towards the end of a small spiral arm.

Or maybe we live in a space hollowed out
by the Holy Hand
on His armrest.

Maybe what we think is a cluster or supercluster of neighboring
galaxies
is an armchair the Almighty moved to a spot
by a window in His mansion.

Maybe this immense, cold and dark universe
is a small space where He stores
cosmic light bulbs
we think are stars.

Is each millennia simply
one breath exhaled?
Are we the only intelligent life
here so the Universe

can know itself in some small way?
Are we specs of cosmic dust,
seen in one flash of light
and gone forever?

We ask these questions. But where did the words come from?

Keep probing the cosmos,
but you won't find the origin of The Word anywhere,
yet we know it is real,
because you are using it this moment!

God is so much bigger than we are,
and so is His love,
and whatever it is,
we truly are in His hands,

and his hands are certainly on the spiral arm
of the Milky Way,
and you can call it what you want,
but I'm calling that
the armrest of the recliner
of God Almighty!

FLAMINGOS

by Tom Josephson

How I love the Flamingos
at the entrance of the zoo
reflecting in your young eyes
in my memory
and the love in my heart bursting
and bursting again
recalling the days of your childhood joy
and my joy hand in hand
father and son
on sunny days
at the zoo
or the park
or pitching baseballs
you were the love of my life

and now you're a man
so strong and good
a policeman and I still love you son,

I love the sound of your voice
and everything about you

every conversation
every single second
of my life with you
has been joy beyond description
and you are still
the love of my life

and I can still see those flamingos
in your eyes.

Epilogue

How Did This Happen?
by Marcia Goranson

A relationship aimed at taking down and dismantling the last stronghold...and it did. Mission accomplished. I found the key, buried in me. Freedom, peace and release all wrapped up together as a gift. Given to me as the words were spoken–'There is nothing wrong with you.' All this time, so many places I've gone, searching for the evasive but underlying truth. To find it finally here in Ryan's Cathedral. The misbeliefs, so hurtful, destructive and confining, have finally been extinguished and laid to rest.

Now, I've found my healing hand, ready to extend. To help others smother and eliminate their own false voices. To annihilate shame and its binding effects, with the fires of truth. Scouring out the infectious mendacity and delusions of evil, planted in the souls of those abused and misused.

Thank you, Lord. The truth wins!

Carry on!

The following is Sophie's handwritten list of relatives and friends lost in the Holocaust.

RELATIVES AND FRIENDS LOST IN THE HOLOCAUST
(ALL THESE PEOPLE I KNEW PERSONALLY)

MY GRANDPARENTS: BEREL & TAMERLA LIEBERMAN - LIVED IN LODZ AND DIED OF
STARVATION IN THE LODZ GHETTO. (THEIR AGE ABOUT 68-70 YRS. OLD)

MY GRANDFATHER: SYMCHA SOLAN - LIVED IN LODZ - DIED OF STARVATION IN THE
GHETTO AT THE END OF 1942. (HE WAS ABOUT 70 YRS. OLD)

UNCLE JOE'S PARENTS: WOLF & RACHEL KLEINBAUM - LIVED IN LODZ AND DIED
OF STARVATION IN THE GHETTO.

MY COUSIN
PHYLLIS' OLDEST SISTER } POLA LIEBERMAN DIED IN AUSCHWITZ CONCENTRATION CAMP.
SHE WAS 26 YRS. OLD. (SHE WAS DEPORTED FROM THE LODZ GHETTO
TOGETHER WITH HER PARENTS AND 2 SISTERS.)

MY FATHER'S UNCLE & DAUGHTER
& HIS WIFE } MEYER & DORA LIEBERMAN AND DAUGHTER FELLA -
LIVED IN LODZ - DIED IN AUSCHWITZ. (FELLA WAS 16 YRS. OLD)

MY MOTHER'S BROTHER,
WIFE & 2 SONS
(ROSE'S FAMILY) } RAFAEL & GLICKSHA SOLAN AND SONS JACOB & GABRIEL.
LIVED IN LODZ - DIED IN AUSCHWITZ. (THE SONS WERE 17 & 19 YRS. OLD)

MY FATHER'S BROTHER-IN-LAW: SRULKE WULZ PLUS HIS 4 CHILDREN.
(MY UNCLE
AND 4 COUSINS) 3 SONS- LEIBEL, CHANEL, CHIEL AND 1 DAUGHTER - CHANA (ALL WERE
IN THEIR 20§) LIVED IN LODZ - DIED IN AUSCHWITZ.

MY FATHER'S COUSINS: SHMUEL & DORA KRONENBERG AND SON ABRAM (ABRAM WAS 18 YRS. OLD)
LIVED IN LODZ - DIED IN AUSCHWITZ

MY FATHER'S COUSINS: MEYER FRYDMAN, WIFE & YOUNG DAUGHTER
LIVED IN LODZ - DIED IN AUSCHWITZ

MY MOTHER'S COUSINS: SHAINA GITEL & WOLF GREENBAUM ALSO
BALACHAJA & ABRAM JACOB   ROCHWERG (ALL IN THEIR 4c
LIVED IN LODZ - DIED IN AUSCHWITZ

MY COUSIN: RUDOLPH KUCHINSKI - LIVED IN BERLIN - ESCAPED TO
BRUSSELS AND WAS KILLED BY THE NAZIS WHEN GERMANY
OVERRAN BELGIUM. HE WAS 20 YRS. old

MY FRIEND: EVA BERGER, HER MOTHER AND SISTER, ETTA - LIVED IN BERLIN -
ESCAPED TO BRUSSELS AND WERE KILLED THERE BY THE NAZIS.
(EVA WAS 17 YEARS & ETTA 19 years old.)

MY PARENTS' FRIENDS: PINCHAS & LEIA PINKUS & THEIR YOUNG SON
LIVED IN BERLIN & DIED IN BUCHENWALD CONCENTRATION
CAMP

MY FATHER'S ~~FRIEND~~ FRIEND LEON PLUTNO & WIFE & DAUGHTER ANNE
AND FAMILY LIVED IN PARIS (WIFE & DAUGHTER WERE BORN IN PARI
DAUGHTER MY AGE
ALL DIED IN DACHAU

MY MOTHER'S COUSINS: SHMUEEK ROCHWERG ALSO GOLDA KUCHINSKI
LIVED IN BRUSSELS WERE KILLED BY THE
NAZIS.

MY FATHER'S FRIEND: REINHART NEUMANN - LIVED IN BERLIN -
ESCAPED TO AMSTERDAM - WAS KILLED BY THE
NAZIS WHEN THEY OVERRAN HOLLAND.

MY COUSIN: RUDOLPH KUCHINSKI - LIVED IN BERLIN - ESCAPED TO
            BRUSSELS AND WAS KILLED BY THE NAZIS WHEN GERMANY
            OVERRAN BELGIUM. HE WAS 20 YRS. old

MY FRIEND: EVA BERGER, HER MOTHER AND SISTER, ETTA - LIVED IN BERLIN -
            ESCAPED TO BRUSSELS AND WERE KILLED THERE BY THE NAZIS.
            (EVA WAS 17 YEARS & ETTA 19 years old.)

MY PARENTS' FRIENDS: PINCHAS & LEIA PINKUS ✓ THEIR YOUNG SON
                LIVED IN BERLIN & DIED IN BUCHENWALD CONCENTRATION
                                    CAMP

MY FATHER'S ~~FRIEND~~ FRIEND LEON PLUTNO & WIFE & DAUGHTER ANNE
AND FAMILY   LIVED IN PARIS (WIFE & DAUGHTER WERE BORN IN PARIS -
                              DAUGHTER MY AGE
            ALL DIED IN DACHAU

MY MOTHER'S COUSINS: SHMULEK ROCHWERG ALSO GOLDA KUCHINSKI
                LIVED IN BRUSSELS WERE KILLED BY THE
                NAZIS.

MY FATHER'S FRIEND: REINHART NEUMANN - LIVED IN BERLIN -
               ESCAPED TO AMSTERDAM - WAS KILLED BY THE
               NAZIS WHEN THEY OVERRAN HOLLAND.

JACK WEISBLACK'S FAMILY: NAME IN POLISH WAS <u>WAJSBLACH</u>
      FATHER - ~~ABRAHAM~~ MOISHE
      MOTHER - SHEINDLA
      SISTER - HELEN
      BROTHER - ABRAHAM
      BROTHER - SALEK

Sophie Lieberman-Josephson 1923 – 2011

Printed in the USA
CPSIA information can be obtained
at www.ICGtesting.com
LVHW02084509082 4
787586LV00014B/597

9 798893 333176